FROM ARTHUR'S SEAT

A COLLECTION OF SHORT
FICTION AND POETRY

From Arthur's Seat

First published by Egg Box Publishing 2017
in partnership with the University of Edinburgh

A CIP record for this book is available from the British Library

Design by Caitlin Malone McLaughlin

Typeset in Cochin, 12pt

Printed and bound in the UK by Imprint Digital

Distributed by Central Books

ISBN: 978-1-911343-15-8

FROM ARTHUR'S SEAT

Editor in Chief   *James J. Valliere*
Cover and Interior Design   *Caitlin Malone McLaughlin*
Financial Officer   *Michael S. Marshall*

Fiction Editors   *Rachana Bhattacharjee*
    Jessica Irish

Poetry Editors   *Celia Wilding*
    Grace Hiu-Yan Wong

Art Coordinators   *James Machell*
    Elvis Sokoli

Interior Artwork   *Victoria Rose Ball*

Readers   *Cassidy Colwell*
    Paula Espinosa Valarezo
    Megan Jones
    Elena Sturk Lussier
    Josh Simpson
    Drew Townsend
    Francesca Vavotici
    Jessica Widner
    Michael Worrell

Special Thanks   *Katie Craig*
    Alan Gillis
    Robert Alan Jamieson
    Jane McKie
    Sam Riviere
    Allyson Stack
    Alice Thompson

TABLE OF CONTENTS

TABLE OF CONTENTS

FOREWORD
Dr. Allyson Stack

You hold in your hands the second issue of Edinburgh University's annual Creative Writing Anthology, *From Arthur's Seat*. The students whose work you are about to read came to this city from near and far to take up their pens and add their own voices to Edinburgh's vibrant chorus. To write in a city whose pubs and steep-pitched roofs once sheltered the likes of Hugh MacDiarmid, Muriel Spark, Robert Burns, and Sorley MacLean (not to mention Stevenson and Scott) is, by turns, a thrilling adventure and a daunting task. It is an act made all the more impressive given the distances most of these writers travelled before ever setting foot in a classroom. They hail from all corners of the earth. From the warm shores of the Bahamas to the slightly chillier ones of Scotland, from Canada, Hong Kong, Greece, Ecuador, Bulgaria, and China, they have all made Edinburgh their home for the past year with one aim in mind—to become better writers. Their diverse biographies, ethnicities, identities, and nationalities shine through every page in this anthology. In one story we find ourselves in the grip of injustice in an Army office in colonial India. In another we are experiencing the devastating aftermath of a father's assassination in Beirut. We go from navigating a crime scene in an unnamed corner of Glasgow to awaking in the confines of a 26th century coffin. A poem might begin in a 'warm motel over Lake Eerie' only to give way to visions and juxtapositions that grow more evocative, fresh, and unhinged with every line.

But even more exciting than the diversity of the writers themselves is the marvelous variety of style, form, and tone. You are about to encounter poems that range from tightly structured haiku to dense unrelenting prose poetry to finely wrought free verse. You will soon read fiction that spans the minimalism of Ray Carver, the palm-of-the-hand sensibility of Kawabata, and the Saunders-esque absurdism of a teenaged boy's travails cast in high chivalric mode. A criticism often levelled at Creative Writing programmes is that they tend to produce over-workshopped, homogenised literary fare. This anthology puts the lie to such a notion. What awaits you is far from bland. Dig in. Enjoy.

SHORT STORIES

Writing Bernadette

Francesca Vavotici

Get ready. This isn't going to be easy, so you better be prepared. You're about to write a novel. It requires focus.

Turn your laptop on. Type your password.

Wait. What's the matter? What have you done? You've skipped a number. You're always going too fast. That's what she'd say. But she's not here anymore. Come on, do it again.

Ah, there we go. You've got it. See that icon on the far left? Click on that. Open a new document. Look at the blank page. Isn't it exciting? And alarming, of course. But you can do it. You know you can.

Press those keys, one at a time. That's right. Why is nothing happening? Oh, this laptop's slow. You should have taken it back to the store. You should have had it fixed. I know you meant to do it, but that's not enough.

There, there. Stop beating yourself up. Nothing you can do now. Just remember to save the file every now and then. You don't want all of your good work to go to waste. You're on a mission here. You do this one small thing, and all your life will fall into place. Don't screw this up.

The Beginning

When I was seven years old, a skinny kid with crooked teeth and permanently messy hair, I met a girl. She was six and pretty, with a small button for a nose and lots of freckles all over her cheekbones. Her name was Bernadette.

We went to school together, and every day during our lunch break we would rush out to the garden and collect leaves. We were building a nest for our friend Pip. Our imaginary friend Pip.

He was a nice chap. Pink and yellow —Bernadette had chosen the colours — with a lime green beak, and he could speak, of course. Bernadette had taught him to rhyme, and that's what he'd always do. I found it a bit annoying, but I never said a thing. You see, apart from Bernadette, he was my only friend.

Hold on a second. This won't do. You want the audience to know who your heroine is. Why the hero finds her so irresistibly attractive. Why he'll fight to the death —or to the end of the novel— to get her back. What is it that makes her special?

Well, yes, there's those big blue eyes. Of course. And the smile. With those perfect rows of teeth and the little dimples hiding in a sea of freckles. Oh, she's beautiful. No doubt about that. And smart. Remember that time she read *Romeo and Juliet* in fifth grade? She paused and sighed in all the right places.

Show the reader how great she is. It shouldn't be difficult. This is not a work of fantasy after all.

Beginning 2.0

As we sat in the garden after school, Bernadette would read Pip poetry. She was teaching him to speak in rhymes. She liked poetry, and art. I think that's maybe why she liked me.

You know, I was very good at composition. The teacher would always compliment me on the detail of my holiday accounts. I even won a prize, once. I think Bernadette must have seen I was destined to do great things.

Now that's ridiculous. Unless you count repairing your mum's kitchen sink in exchange for free rent as a 'great thing.' In which case, you're absolutely right, and I apologise.

Seriously though, tone it down.

Beginning 2.1

She liked poetry and art. I think that's maybe why I got into all of this stuff in the first place.

It's not that I didn't like it, but I certainly wasn't passionate about it until I met Bernadette. And maybe even now, I don't care so much. Do you hear me? I don't give a crap if this is good. I DO NOT GIVE A SHIT.

Right. I wouldn't want to discourage you, but this is obviously not going terribly well. Why don't you take a break? Stretch your legs. Have a chocolate. Chocolate makes everything better. When she left you, that's all you did for a week. Ate chocolate. It made all the difference, didn't it?

You know, maybe you should start from the ending. That's what the greatest writers do, one step at a time.

Chapter 22

It's been two years since I saw Bernadette for the last time. She said she couldn't deal with me anymore. That I was a failure. Then, she walked out the door and never looked back. Gone, forever. Or, at least, that's what I thought.

I was walking down High Street one Sunday morning, hunting for inspiration for my next bestseller, when I saw her looking at the window of a souvenir shop. She was so beautiful. I remembered every moment together, strolling down a park hand in hand or sitting at a café drinking frappuccinos and laughing at silly jokes. Could we ever have that again?

I knew it would be hard. But I had to try.

That's it? That's the ending? Oh well, she'd be delighted to know that once again you're being... What was that word again? 'Vague'? 'Indecisive'?

'Inconclusive.' Yes, that's it. Inconclusive. She's surely going to fall in love with you all over again if you show her you haven't changed one bit. After all, she clearly didn't know what she was doing when she left you. She probably spent the past two years pining for you.

Sure, you saw her in Waterstones hand in hand with a guy, but that could have been her gay best friend. Because really, all she's ever wanted is you.

Is this what you think? Wake up, you idiot. If you want this, if you *really* want this, you've got to make it happen. Don't be yourself. Yourself is useless. Be the person she wanted you to be. Get back to that page and prove to her you're worth it.

when I saw her looking at the window of a souvenir shop. She was so beautiful. I took a deep breath and started walking towards...

What's that noise? That buzzing. Shut up for a second. Listen. It's coming from the bed. What the hell is it?

Oh, your phone. Look at the screen. Who is it?

No, it can't be. It's impossible. Have you willed this into being? Have you got superpowers now?

'Hello?'

Stop cracking your knuckles. She can hear you. You know it drives her crazy.

'Hi Jim.'

'H-hi.'

'Long time no hear.'

Well yes, but that's okay, right? Tell her. Tell her it's okay. Tell her you're glad she called.

'Yep.'

'Well, how are you?'

Shocked? Speechless? On the verge of a nervous breakdown?

'Good.'

'Well, I'm glad. What have you been up to?'

Oh, she's interested. She's hoping you've got your shit together. She'll probably want to see you. She'll be so proud. You'll take her to get Indian. She loves it. She'll probably ask you to move straight back in. This is great.

'I've — I've been writing, actually.'

'Oh really? That's brilliant, Jim.'

See? You've got this.

'Yeah, I've been writing a novel —'

'Listen, Jim. There's something I've got to tell you.'

She's missed you. She can't live without you. Come back home.

'I'm getting married.'

She's getting — No. Wait a second. Just, wait. This is not happening. It's just not. This is your story. You're the author. Shut this down.

She was so beautiful. I stood there, looking at her for as long as I could. Her freckles, her soft hair, her pale skin. She never turned. She never saw me.

As she walked away, a ray of sunshine broke through the clouds, its light reflecting on something on her finger. A ring.

13

The sight hurt my eyes. I looked away.

I traced my steps back to North Bridge. I could see a train approaching in the distance. I leaned from the parapet, wondering what it would feel like. Not to jump, but to let myself fall. To stop resisting and just drop down.

The train was gathering speed. I took a deep breath and stepped back. Too spineless to even die.

The End

Wow, that sure sounds cheerful. You know what? You're not in the mood today.

Get up. Grab your lucky blanket. Stop pretending you don't have a lucky blanket. I know you do. Grab it, now. Do you feel better, cuddled into a knitted cocoon? I thought so. How about a little online shopping? Or some therapeutic baking? You could make those amazing chocolate and orange cookies. Oh, you're right. That's Bernadette's recipe. You don't want to think about that.

Maybe you don't want to think at all? Well, the good news is now you have devices that do that for you. Turn on that smart TV. Click on the Netflix icon. *Crazy Ex-Girlfriend*. Well, that sounds about right.

CHRISTOPHER ST.
Elvis Sokoli

Jessica waits at the Christopher St. stop for the Downtown 2 to Brooklyn.

Despite a 1 in 20 million chance of her perishing in an act of terror, she persists with imagining the worst. These thoughts strike her without warning, often passing in a flash but sometimes maintaining a hold on her imagination long enough to become unsettling. Tonight, on a crowded subway platform, yet another terror thought invades: a remote detonation.

A quarter hour before, she was struggling through a happy hour Merlot with a regrettable Bumble date at her favorite wine bar on 8th Street. After her date's third mention of his high-salaried job, she laughed at how she'd prefer a terror attack at that moment. Unfortunately, her laugh coincided with her date's joke about a business conquest. He squeezed her left hand with confidence as a result.

'Would you like to come back to my place to check out my vinyl collection?' he said.

'I would prefer not to,' she said.

Her fifth consecutive dating app date, had she really sunk so low as to depend on a series of left and right swipes when looking for love? But a prolonged meditation on modern dating is a luxury she cannot afford while looking out for suspicious characters. A liberal, Jessica doesn't profile; but a man on the other side of the platform sports a shaved head, long beard, shades, and a backpack clutched to his chest as he vigorously shakes his right leg. This certainly warrants her attention.

The Downtown 2 to Brooklyn will arrive in ten minutes.

Emil left his advisor's office downtrodden but composed after his thesis proposal, a sketch-essay documenting New York through its inhabitants' feet, was dismissed. 'I hate to say this,' Professor Kleeman said, 'but it reminds me of a poorly executed, podophelic *Humans of New York* knockoff.'

The walk from Kleeman's office to the Christopher St. stop resulted in twenty minutes of anger, self-doubt, and self-loathing. Transitioning from self-doubt to self-loathing, tears penetrated Emil's earlier composure. He pictured how pathetic he might've seemed: a grown man with a beautiful beard and chest hair, crying, walking down 6th Ave.

Sad.

He masked his shameful swollen eyes by throwing on sunglasses well after sunset.

He sits waiting for the Uptown 1 to The Bronx at the Christopher St. stop.

Emil's girlfriend, Sarah, is working late, so he'll have enough time to make himself decent and regain his manhood. He's sensitive. But he's an artist. A touch of raw emotion bandied about goes a long way. That's what originally attracted Sarah to him. He longs to hug her waist, head in her lap, her fingers rubbing his bald head, as she reassures him that it will be okay, that many geniuses are misunderstood at first. He clutches his bag to his chest and struggles to control his leg from shaking. Even his daydreams are unbecoming. Is he a misunderstood genius?

The Uptown 1 to The Bronx will arrive in ten minutes.

Emil places his backpack on the platform floor in between his legs. He unzips the bag and pulls out an iPad. He opens the file titled 'Tread All Over Me: The Feet Walking New York' to examine his thesis proposal. Some beautiful feet. The best feet. Immigrant feet, women's feet, tourists' feet, his feet, Sarah's feet: New Yorker feet. He really does have a knack for sketching feet, for really drawing life into them, every vein so articulated, so — life-like? Emil swiped through each page with careful precision, taking his time to examine every detail. He felt a warm rush spread through his body. Why couldn't Kleeman see what he could, what Sarah could, what his mother could? Because those who can't do, teach etc etc? He'll be damned if he allows a failed artist to judge his potential.

He leaves his bag unattended under the bench, iPad in hand, looking for the estimated arrival time for the Uptown 1 to The Bronx.

Emil is unaware that on the opposite platform stands an old friend, fixing her undivided attention on whom she presumes to be a random subway passenger in need of having his threat level assessed. Jessica doesn't realise the man who abandoned his backpack is Emil, a high school friend, and not a potential terrorist preparing to detonate remotely the bomb in his bag using his iPad.

Both the Downtown 2 and the Uptown 1 will arrive in five minutes.

Why does Jessica subject herself to riding the subway if her terror anxiety persists? Death drive? Perhaps. But it's most likely due to the rising costs of taxis and Uber and because she's making $15/hr, has considerable student loans and literally lives in a refurbished tool-shack with two roommates. Concessions are necessary. But will she say something now that she's seen something or thinks she's seen something? Or is her unwillingness (inability?) to report what she (thinks she) sees as a death sentence for those around her? She's frozen with responsibility. Maybe she should have accepted her date's offer to see his vinyl collection.

On the walk back to his seat, Emil notices a fascinating pair of feet in flip-flops. Veiny, calloused, hairy, dirty, tired. There would be no better image for the cover art of his final work. His artistic drive urges him forward. With only a few minutes before his train arrives, Emil hastens to his seat, puts away his iPad, and retrieves a notebook and a pencil. Advisors are replaceable; great art isn't.

Surely now that the man has returned to his seat, put away his iPad, and begun to draw, Jessica and her fellow New Yorkers are safe. The unkempt beard, the shaved head hiding a vastly receded hairline, the all-black attire, sun glasses below ground and beat up Chucks — he looks more like a pretentious art student than a suspicious character.

Both the Downtown 2 and the Uptown 1 will arrive in two minutes.

As Jessica examines Emil, she makes no attempt to avert her gaze. As Emil tries to get a better look of the man's feet he's sketching, he takes off his sunglasses, hangs them off his v-neck, and stares up and ahead across the platform. Emil and Jessica's eyes meet and divert just as fast.

A strange feeling of familiarity overcomes them both. Unable to place exactly what inspires this nostalgia, they sneak a discreet peek without giving themselves away. But the attempt is unsatisfactory for both parties.

Their respective trains approach; Jessica moves to the front of her platform, Emil to his. He puts his sunglasses on so as to watch her covertly, and he finally places her; seeing Emil approach the front of his platform, about to put on his sunglasses, they lock eyes again and the memory clicks: the last time Jessica saw him he looked more like a boy than a suspicious character.

That was eight years ago. They were close enough throughout

high school, making out a few times sophomore year, partnering in Model UN three consecutive years, had frequent coffee dates, and an unabashed comfort level where they could discuss anything. They considered each other good friends. And although their last time seeing one another was at a house party after the first semester of college, they kept in touch, through texts, then Facebook, before their friendship dwindled down to liking social media posts every so often and thinking of the other with less and less frequency. The last time they interacted was five years ago on Facebook. Emil liked Jessica's post where she shared a video of cats jumping at the sight of cucumbers. He soon thereafter quit social media following a self-righteous rant about the degradation of culture. Jessica didn't notice his lack of an online presence for months.

They accept they've recognised the other, unaware if the other has recognized them in turn. They think of each other for the first time in years. What rendered their friendship irrelevant? And why didn't they say anything there? They resist a last glance before entering their respective trains. They dreaded the experience. Would they have hollered across the platforms at each other? Waved their arms like people stranded on a desert island, hoping to catch the attention of an overhead plane or a faraway ship? It'd have been absurd.

But with a high school reunion approaching, Emil's studying Downtown, Jessica's working Downtown, their reliance on the Christopher St.-Sheridan Sq. subway home, irrespective of different lines, directions, they were bound to meet again, not by destiny but circumstance and proximity. On the train, Emil pauses his artistic urge and thinks maybe he should get back on Facebook. Jessica pulls a Murakami paperback from her purse. She struggles, but manages to shake away thoughts of a sarin strike as statistically improbable. She looks out the window at Emil's train, having left before hers, noticing the ghastly qualities of the passengers' faces dissolving into the tunnel.

THE SURGEON, THE PATIENT, AND THE PARASITE

Yutong Fu

I am an optical surgeon. Every day, my work starts precisely at eight o'clock. When I put on the white robe and sterilised gloves, the routine of operation after operation waits for me until late into the night. I am a skilled surgeon, popular, wealthy. People in high positions ask me to treat their family members and friends, and I am never in want of women's company. I possess a skill that removes others' pain, a beneficial career. My colleagues often talk about me in whispers, 'That guy is so bloody lucky. What more could he ask for?' All that I can be sure of is that I do not feel happy about my life, but I do not feel unhappy, either. Instead, I always feel I am drowning in the lake of blankness, suffocated by the endless sense of emptiness. My house is big, my car expensive. My life flows like a pink stream, warm, comfortable, smooth as silk, yet I see neither sparkles nor gleams. I cannot feel the exhaustion of my work, or the pain of my patients, because for me, these are unreal, as if covered by the veil of dream. The only real feeling I own is the acute sense of blankness, devouring me inch by inch, like bacteria decaying teeth.

One day, a patient was suddenly assigned to me. He was a man of middle age, skin as yellow as a dead leaf. His left eye bulged out of the socket, and the eyelid could barely cover it, leaving a crevice from which yellowish exudation glistened malignantly. The other eye was completely blank, staring steadily forward.

'There's a parasite in his eye,' said an old woman who accompanied him, handing me the X-ray photograph and pointing at his bulging eye. I nodded. The patient wore a numb face, as if the situation had nothing to do with him, and he was just a ghost who happened to float into the hospital.

'Does it hurt?' I asked my patient, because he did not show any sign of pain.

'Yes, it hurts,' the patient answered, in a none-of-my-business tone, 'Sometimes I feel that the parasite is not only chewing my eye, but chewing my very soul as well.'

The old woman shuddered, but the patient just sneered, and continued, 'At first, I yelled; I rolled on the ground; I broke everything I laid my hands on. You have no idea how acute the pain is. It's like all the blood becomes solid, scratching the veins; all bones chopped to powder; all flesh torn open by the beaks of vultures. I would be glad, incredibly glad, to see myself burnt alive to ashes. I would love to see the lovely flames dancing upon my carcass. But suddenly one day, the pain stopped. It disappeared, or more likely, it melted into my very being, as if it had always been there since I came into this world. From then on, instead of pain, I felt a suffocating numbness, as if someone was covering my eyes, my nose, my mouth, my ears with cotton; all my senses were lost. I can't breathe, unless I embrace the pain. But now even the pain itself is not painful anymore. Emptiness, complete emptiness, almost drives me mad, as if someone wants to suffocate me in my quilt.'

'He's lost his mind, doctor,' the old woman explained hastily. 'I hope you don't mind.'

'Not at all, I will do everything in my power to help him,' I said. 'I'm glad to hear what he just said.' I wanted to add, 'It relieved me a great deal.'

The next day, when I stepped into the operating room, the patient was lying still upon the operating table, anaesthetised. His eyes were wide open, staring at the ceiling he could not see. Composedly, I picked up the bistoury and slit open the epithelium, as I had done thousands of times before. The muscle in the eyeball twitched violently. Though the patient's mind was unconscious, his body could still sense the pain. My mask covered my sneer. The chill in my eyes, like a malicious freezing light, must have shot through my glasses, for I perceived that my assistant, though just for a second, shrank uneasily. Little by little, I dug into the morbid eyeball, probing for the parasite. The yellowish emission kept seeping out, like a snake hissing out venom. It mingled with blood, and dyed my gloves brown, the colour of the parasite's malignance.

'I know how you must feel, locked in such a disgusting flesh ball, and squashed,' I said silently to the parasite, 'I can sense your hatred and repulsion bursting out of this flesh-prison, intensified by the knowledge that you have to rely on it, no matter how it disgusts you. Yet your pain pleases me, as well as the pain you have caused.' Suddenly, I felt a slight vibration passing through my bistoury, and I could perceive a tiny white spot wriggling. Stealthily, I approached it with tweezers, and caught it firmly in a precise attack. Slowly, I drew it out, while appreciating the agony of the twitching eyeball. How fast it twitched, as if the eyeball itself had turned into a fat restless bug. When the parasite was pulled completely out of the eyeball, the patient, still unconscious, sighed with relief, and I was perfectly sure that when he woke up, he would become the kindhearted good-tempered man he used to be, and the madness he showed before the operation would soon be forgotten. I did not loosen my grasp on the tweezers, and leaving the suture to my assistants, I took the parasite to the sterilisation room next door.

Lighting an alcohol lamp, I closely observed the parasite. It was thin, transparent, about 1mm in diameter, 20cm in length, still curling elegantly upon the tweezers, gleaming in the light of the fire. Steadily, I put the tweezers upon the flame. The parasite caught fire, cracking, shrivelling, a sound like treading upon dead twigs, with tiny golden sparks flying. The sound and smell of burning satisfied me, as if I had just enjoyed a full-body massage, all my rigid joints relaxed. As I watched this execution, a sense of fulfillment was finally bestowed upon me.

HIS NAME WAS THE TURTLE

Paula Espinosa Valarezo

They called him The Turtle, mostly because he was a slow walker, but also because he seemed to have a shell on his back. This was true in two ways: he had a terrible hump which made him look like a turtle and he seemed to be impossible to harm. While walking, he would always have his hands on his chest and his chin touching his collar bone, and all you could see was his shelly hump. Rumour has it that he was actually a very handsome man when he was young, and that this building has been his home for more than 40 years. But no one could verify the story, no one knew where he came from. It was not that he was ugly now, he just wasn't a man, he was a turtle. The way he moved through the corridor was almost like swimming; it was impossible to hear him coming, he always caught you by surprise. Someone said that he got the nickname from a boy who used to live in the building. The boy just looked at him once and knew he was a turtle. The nickname stuck, even when families moved away and new people came in. His name was The Turtle.

No one had seen the interior of his apartment, all anyone knew was that he used to live on the 10th floor and then he moved to the ground floor, almost as if he was running away from the colossal mountains haunting his windows. 'He wanted to be closer to the beach,' the doorman said once. The only remarkable thing about his home was the constant sound of running water. He never gave any explanation about this, nor did anyone care enough to raise the question.

He never talked to anybody, never shared the lift, never engaged in any kind of social gathering, and you might even say he actively avoided children. People in the building believed he cried a lot, as he had a piercing smell of salt. It had to be tears, some said, as they believed The Turtle never sweat. He had built some sort of structure on the little patio in his apartment, and if you walked past the back of the building, you could see the structure and a bluish light coming out of it. Some said that if you walked past it during the colder months, it was possible to feel the warmth coming out of it, and sometimes, the moisture.

People love to talk, and some said that he never did the paperwork to build a pool, but that he did it anyway inside his secret structure. Others said that he was one of those grow-your-own-food kind of guys. This made sense, considering you rarely saw him with any groceries, except for gallons and gallons of water. As the rumours became more and more detailed, they started to pay more attention to The Turtle. He was alone, that was certain. No signs of a spouse or kids, and no friends. However, there was something about The Turtle that made a family man out of him. He looked like one of those grandfathers that could spend all day telling stories about their huge families. But The Turtle was alone, swimming quietly in his apartment.

His skin was particularly green, but then, all old people have awful skin. His eyes were yellow, not honey, not amber, not hazel: yellow. Not that it was easy to notice, as his huge and wrinkled eyelids made it almost impossible to look him in the eye. Besides, he had a deep-sea mood around him.

I first heard about The Turtle when the sand appeared. I had recently moved into the building and had no interest in getting to know my neighbours. They were all whispering outside of The Turtle's apartment, as loud as whispers can go. I tried to walk right past them, and then I saw the sand. Apparently, he didn't open the door. Most of the neighbours felt that someone owed them an explanation, but he just wouldn't open the door. Over the next few days, the smell coming out of his apartment became so intense that it was impossible to ignore. It smelled like the beach, salty and warm.

The following morning, a beam of bluish light was sneaking out of his barely open door. I don't know what got into me, but I just walked in. He was sitting in a kiddie pool full of water, and the smell of salt made my eyes itch. His house was all wet, and the walls and floor were covered in beautiful green and blue tiles. There was sand everywhere, a little piece of beach in the middle of this mountain town. He looked at me in silence, I closed the door behind me and took my shoes off. I sat on the sand and closed my eyes, it had been a while since my last trip to the beach. He explained to me that he was guarding his eggs.

Turtle hatchlings are delicate, most of them don't make it to the sea, and some others are eaten before they can even try to get to the water. No words were needed, The Turtle's efforts were not in vain, the eggs were his priority, and nothing could happen to them.

So I kept his secret and even helped him with the warmth, the sand and the salty water, just as he wanted. Yet we both realised this was not going to work, we couldn't keep the sand as warm and salty. The moment was getting closer, but we couldn't reproduce the sounds of the waves, or scavenging seagulls flying in circles. We could both feel the plan breaking into pieces.

I woke up one night at 3:00 am, took The Turtle and his eggs, and made haste to the beach. He didn't say a word for the entire six-hour drive, but I could see him changing as we got closer to the coast. His skin became greener and a bit scaly, his hump grew harder, and I saw his arms shrink and stretch as if wanting to exchange the mitt for the fin, as if wanting to swim. It took us a while to find a desolate beach for the eggs, but the spot he chose was perfect. The sand was white and sparkling, and the water the calmest and bluest I had ever seen. He made all the arrangements, dug a hole in the sand, and put his belly to it, his cold body chilling the sand. The Turtle rested.

Not much time had passed when the cracks began. In the blink of an eye, the little creatures were finding their way to the ocean, swimming through the sand. My eyes, full of tears, couldn't believe the scene. I took one or two in my hands and showed them the right path. They all knew exactly what to do when they touched the water. I turned around, I wanted to see The Turtle. When I did, he looked small and dried up. I took his heavy body and put it in the water. It began to sink slowly, as if he belonged in the bottom of the sea. I heard his fins flapping in the distance.

His name was The Turtle.

THE RUINS (A DREAM)

Jessica Widner

Far away, a woman she used to be is dreaming of a house with many rooms. She walks through them, touches the curtains. The house is empty.

Here, she sits at the end of all things, out in the sun at least, which keeps her face warm, the rest of her wrapped up in fur. Next to her a man in a wheelchair breathes loudly through tubes connected to a glass cylinder, invisible forces cleaning the air he inhales, stripping it of toxins. He has the face of a young man, but his shoulders and hands are fragile and curled.

They sit on a high balcony, over the immobile ocean. Under them a high wave has reared up and frozen.

I used to be surrounded by things, she says out loud. The sun reflects off the ice. All is very bright. He acts as though he hasn't heard her. She repeats herself, louder this time. He meets her eyes. Yes, his eyes say, I know exactly what you mean.

His eyes are dark and they don't reflect the light. Other than that his face is lovely, only because, right now, it looks very young. She likes having someone to sit with, but she hates his breathing machine, and the scraping noise it makes. It makes her think of a wounded animal, or a baby born premature, the thing lying in the space between living and dying. She thinks of taking the tubes from his nose. Would he die? What would that look like? Would his eyes ascend first? Would his body follow? Or would he sink, would the water begin to move again?

She has begun to think beyond the body. She has begun to think about things that will never happen. Physical impossibilities. This is what happens when there is no sound in the world. Yes, there are the tubes. There is *noise*. There is no sound. Things stretch on white and jagged. There are mountains, all around them like walls.

Oh my god! she raises her voice. Oh my god! she says again, and then: I've lost absolutely everything.

He shakes his head. He doesn't speak. She imagines what he would (what he *should*) say, if he could speak:

No (he'd say), No, you didn't lose everything, because that would have been careless of you. You're not a careless person (he'd reach out and take her wrist and despite their frail appearance his fingers would feel warm and strong). You're not a careless woman. What happened was, everything was taken away from you. They took the birdlike dreams that beat inside your temples at night (he would now let her wrist go and throw his newly-strong hands in the air to gesture to the invisible evil around them), they took these things and held them in their hands and pulled them, picked them apart until everything was gone, everything that was important or had meaning, was gone, and then there you were, just you, one body, old and empty here at the very end of the world, with me.

Don't you care, she says out loud, don't you care that we're here together? Don't you care at all?

Maybe he looks at her. Maybe he looks downwards.

Time passes, she murmurs, time passes, and here we are.

In a sun-dappled terrace, high in the mountains, on the second day of their honeymoon, she and her new husband are fighting. I don't care, he says, his hand low on her belly, I want both of you.

Her hands clench around the arms of her chair, the tips of her fingernails in her palms with sadness she can't give voice to. You should care, she says, what kind of man are you that you don't care? The day around them is soft and warm, secluded, bird-filled. There is a bottle of wine between them. There is a bottle of wine, and there is an unborn baby that is not his.

You're always angry, he says, looking down at his hands instead of at her face. And then, he does a terrible thing, he laughs at her. Laughing, he leans over to put his arm around her shoulder and pull her towards him. So angry, he says, laughing. Look where we are. Smile. Look at this place. These mountains? Out of sight.

Like a child she does what he asks, the skin of her face feeling loose as if she is about to shed it. It becomes a refrain every time, their marriage chorus: why are you so angry?

Because I made a mistake, she says, from her world of ice, though she knows he, happy, ignorant, stupid in his sunlit paradise, cannot hear her. Because I thought that I needed you.

He laughs at her, because he thinks he did nothing wrong.

Here, smaller than ever, shrinking into his chair, he looks like he is trying to speak.

Do you need the damn tubes? she says, Do you need the damn thing? The air here is clean and cold, isn't it? I hate you not talking to me. I hate this version of you. You disgust me.

She has never wanted to take the tubes from his nose more than she does now, even if it means his death. His face no longer looks young. It folds into itself. He is old now, like her. It was just a trick of the light, a trick of memory.

They have to go inside. She pushes his chair, wheeling him into this strange home which begins as a long, high-ceilinged hall and ends as a cramped apartment, with just a bed, a chair, a bathroom, and a dresser in which they keep the only possessions they have left, a few items of clothing. Even though the room is not far, she is tired by the time she gets there. Soon you will have to wheel me, she tells him.

He falls asleep in his chair. She lies down until sleep comes and she dreams of a woman far away, dancing the Rite of Spring and in the dream she sees it is herself, and she realises she is not dreaming but has instead become that woman again, and yes, she had forgotten, the bud of a child within her, tiny and fishlike. He sits in the lighting booth watching her, under her spell, but why? She looks just like all the other ballerinas.

She hopes her daughter is somewhere warm, wearing the sun like sleeves.

Later, either still under the spell of sleep or not (how should she know?) she walks out under a sky filled with light, stars being born and dying at fantastically accelerated speed, a sky making love to itself. She wants to leap across that frozen ocean, she wants to fly to that place where she is sleeping, twenty-five years old and pregnant and she wants to take that woman in her arms and rock her to sleep the same way that woman will, in three months' time, rock the little girl curled within her to sleep. She wants to whisper the lullabies she sang her daughter to herself, so when the time comes, the words roll off her tongue, although she can't recall ever learning them. So close now she can see her, in front of her, holding her arms out.

Does she dream or, waking, does she conjure her like a film projected?

The woman in front of her shrugs, her face on the lip of laughter and then she waves her away like smoke and she is gone. The lights in the sky have dimmed now. It is dark and, she guesses, cold. Around her the ocean stretches armed with icy spikes. But she walks and breathes freely enough and looks out over the patio, decorated with stone sculptures of woman, one holding a water jug, a harp, a bunch of grapes, a scale.

The landscape then must be false. A life-size diorama of the Ice Age. To someone behind her, human, or statue, or air, or dust, she says:

But if I could will myself to freeze, I would.

It is not cold. The ice is an illusion, or maybe she was never

31

there in the first place, maybe she lies in a bed dreaming, feverish with age. Either way, she walks, slowly, with her bad back and bad knees, back to the little apartment, to the bed where a very old man sleeps soundly, undisturbed by her absence, or by any absence at all.

THREE AISLES
Michael S. Marshall

And a moment later all those things were eclipsed – cut off by the authoritarian sensors that rule the sliding doors of supermarket chains. The closing of the doors gave her purpose: find and gather food. She brushed a strand of long hair back from her face, her other hand by her side, taut, balancing the crooked cage-like basket that was perched in the crux of tendon and joint. Having preceded rush hour by precious minutes, she knew a flood of other shoppers would follow behind her and stepped lively toward the produce aisle. As her footfalls fell, she savoured the seclusion proffered by her timeliness. Like a good mammal, she wanted snacks – healthy. Her eyes flickered among the foliage at the end of the first aisle but rounding the pillar she was confronted with a choice.

Nature was sorted here, crammed in boxes, pruned, bones picked for the good stuff. An array of choices denied to Neolithic man. The shelves, the slats, the artificial chambers felt clinical. Fluorescent overhead lights hollowed eyes and drained living colour from the organic. The pallor sought her ears as well, in the monotone hum of industrial refrigeration. If she were able to look down to her feet, to fight her forward-fixed eyes, to contemplate the scent of vegetation in a sterile environment, she would notice the beige speckled floor – linoleum or some similar such substance carrying a simulacrum of texture; the pattern, dots, on its surface hinted at tarmac, gravel, a fine sand beach, but the hints fall short as no beach is so uniform. If she could tear her mind from the choice before her, looking down, the floor's unreality would only be affirmed by the flicker of a barcode-reader's laser torpefying its surface, inexplicably far-flung from its source, and absentmindedly fired at her feet by an inattentive cashier.

Instead, she looked only at two boxes, chest height. In the left a carrot, in the right an orange – both drawing her eyes and awaiting the company of a pre-rush restock. A sickening grip coalesced in her gut.

Cold air from the butchery and frozen food section was caught on a draft as the sliding doors opened to admit yet another customer – the scent of cool, dead flesh crawled up into the mucus of her nose.

Carrot or orange? Consumers were beginning to flit past her with rising urgency; the beeps of the laser-wielding cashier's scans came at quickening intervals. With each admission granted by the sliding doors the anxiety of the world outside washed in and flooded her thoughts. The carrot: healthy, goes with hummus, carotene is good for eye-sight (?), guests prefer sweet snacks, what if someone comes round? No invites, it'd be unannounced, uninvited and you couldn't feed them (?), what would they think? – orange is better, but that'd waste the hummus, in the fridge, not on the counter, you didn't leave it out did you? Or the stove on? Gas leak (?) – Hummus keeps for a while, maybe (?), why not get both? Greedy? No. Wasteful? Yes. Job, weekend, trip, packing. Carrots keep – why not get both? Are they both organic?

The tang of pesticides danced on her tongue. She felt like she'd drunk some.

(*food* is organic) Is it ethical? Poisonous (?), environment,

34

home grown? Home, home, 'home', misplaced nationalism? A function of mass scale industrialised industry? Would you be collapsing the livelihood of a poor Mediterranean farmer? – or feeding the corrupt corporate interests in increasingly mechanised agriculture? You know this (do you?), you've been here before – you've thought about this, that's why you (researched) chose this supermar– etiquette (workplace conditioning), shopping etiquette? Self-aware (?), you're acting weird.

Each glance the cashier shot bored through her.

They think you have an eating disorder (?), you're thin, you can't pick food, you can't pick the plump orange (lightly bruised) – orange, garish, vitamin C, the juice, the skin, under your nails, in your cuticles, dirty nails garnished with – garnish goes in alcohol; you're hungover, your hair's a mess, you're not, they think you are, you drink too much, you haven't showered (they think), you don't drink enough – at parties (?), guests prefer sweet snacks, think about the orange (or the carrot) not about yourself, your ego (lightly bruised?), you're narcissistic? Narcissus – Greek? Ignorant – *focus*, the carrot (and the orange), you're taking too long, you're taking, too, long– why not buy both why not buy both why not buy – waste.

She felt like a passenger on an airbus. This was an engine failure. She stalled. The plane pitched and fluttered, and as it dived, it would float weightless, helpless. Fluorescent lights would flicker, the beep from the cockpit would go on and on, the hum of artificial noise would give way to the rush of air. A myriad of things, people, belongings, would drift without gravity as they plummeted to earth. A crippling lightness as the listless fuselage sought the ground, an overture to its obliteration, time halts, and floating before her, among all these things, would be an orange and a carrot.

Standing in the aisle, terror lasted only a second longer. She hadn't heard the soft whisper of the plastic bag, but a beautiful limb cut across her, between her and the produce. A hand, its fingers stretching in their translucent veil to engulf the orange. A second hand, the second of the pair, in one deft flicker of movement, smooth, careful, caressing, turning the bag inside out, swathed the orange, passing it into a silken cradle, sealing it inside. The hands were a woman's, confident, kind, forgiving, adorned with polymerised nails and soft skin. They swept away the orange, swinging gaily from the soft pads of forefingers before disappearing around the end of the aisle. In the wake of the orange's departure, panic faded, trepidation drew back into the foliage, and she was awash with relief.

She was calm in the neatly ordered rows, the clear signposts, the descriptive packaging, the consistency of brand and supplier that adorned the shelves like yule decorations in a mead-hall. Her crisis had ended. With the smallest of tremors, she took the carrot and nestled it, swathed in silken plastic, in the firm net-like metal basket. The basket remained secure in the crease of her fingers as it smoothly gyrated through the supermarket aisles, taking whatever more she gave it, and by the time she returned to the scrutinous eyes of the cashier her movements were wholly purposeful and sure. She stood in the wordlessly regimented line and money traded masters with the grace of a well-oiled machine. Finally, with the minute flourish of a soft gust dappled in her hair, the watchful eye of the automatic doors released her into the world. The escaping air, like a draft between pews, met the relief that sighed across her dormant tongue.

As she passed into the free air, her thoughts lingered a moment on the intercession in the produce aisle; she smiled at that divine hand, god from the machine, the orange-taker, in all its ignorance, it had handed her freedom. Freedom from choice.

SUSPICIOUS PACKAGES
Josephine A.

À Montmartre, le 29 décembre 2016

Mon Cher Frédérique,

It's been a while since I wrote to you. These days you seem to be further and further away, and honestly, I think I just missed you. It started on the bus to Saarbrücken. The journey there was torturous. Élodie wouldn't talk to me and time seemed to stand still. All I could think about was reaching Saarbrücken and getting on our train to Paris as soon as possible. You see, Luxembourg wasn't what we'd hoped it'd be. I mean no one in their right mind would ever expect Luxembourg to be amazing and save their miserable lives. Why would we have ever chosen to go there, of all places, for Christmas, if we didn't expect the end of our relationship? In retrospect, I should have seen it coming. And I know it's not Luxembourg's fault. I don't know why I pick on it. Maybe because it's small.

I don't think I've written to you about Élodie. We met ages ago at Elarif's party, but neither of us remembered. We met again two years ago at Piano Vache. Elarif reintroduced us. She didn't catch my eye then either, but she talked to me and at the time all I needed was to listen. She talked to me, talked at me, talked me into things and into her. She talked away the silence.

Six months later I saw her. Not Élodie. The other her. Odile. She was coming out of a boulangerie, breathtaking as always. She lit her cigarette, but by the second puff she got into the car that had just stopped in front of her. I was across the street. She didn't see me. She just smiled at the driver and put her cigarette in his mouth. He smoked and drove away. She took with her all the voices I've been gathering and left me there defenceless once again. And Élodie knew. When I met her that night, I think she knew the moment she saw me that I was hollow again, like the day she met me. But she talked again and she didn't seem to mind then. But you know me. Silence gets to me one way or another. And I understand. You can't keep talking endlessly to a person who doesn't generate any sound of his own.

Luxembourg was a Hail Mary, if you don't know how to pray. Europe isn't to be trusted these days. We were there three days and we happened upon two closed off areas because of suspicious packages. In situations like those, Élodie used to get scared and hold my hand, but in Luxembourg she wasn't scared anymore. She was angry. She said that she couldn't live like that anymore. What if one of them went off? What if one of them hurt her? She'd had enough. I'd gotten used to it. She said that I didn't know how to live any other way. But she did and she didn't want to keep on wasting her life with me. Me, who lived passively in fear of everything. Me, who self-exploded so quietly with no casualties, but his own self. Me, who was lost and didn't want to be found. She said she couldn't keep searching for me. She couldn't keep talking at me. She couldn't keep trying on her own. She just couldn't make it right. Not what you did, not what Odile did when she drove away the first time. She said she didn't want us to be together anymore and got on the bus. I couldn't blame her. She'd put up with me long enough.

All we had to endure was a bus ride and a train ride and then she wouldn't have to see me again. But I told you that Europe isn't to be trusted. When we finally got to Saarbrücken, the train station was closed down and surrounded by police. We asked a German lady what was happening and for someone who doesn't speak very good English she got across the gist of it very well.

'Big bomb,' was all she said. Élodie spoke only to random people trying to get more information and among broken French and basic English we gathered that somebody had called the station letting them know there was a bomb. How nice of them to call. We waited for two hours outside in the cold until they opened the train station again, only to find out that even though all the other trains were delayed, ours was cancelled. The woman at the information desk said that everything was fine. She gave us a hotel room to spend the night and two tickets for the first train to Paris the next morning. We don't think they found a bomb.

The room had two single beds. Élodie changed into her pajamas in the bathroom. It was the most peculiar feeling. I didn't have the right to see her undress anymore. I knew her back was in pain from her bag, but I didn't have the right to do anything about it. I heard her cry and I couldn't hug her. I changed in the bathroom too. I thought it was only fair. There, as I washed my face, I realised that you've been on my mind for a while. Maybe because I got a glimpse of you in the mirror. For a split second you were there and then you were gone. And I felt it. I missed you, brother. And I missed her even if she was right outside my door. Especially because she was right outside my door. But I couldn't go outside. She was right there and yet she was so unreachable. I have found that silence is the longest distance between two people. But she wouldn't speak to me and I can't keep it away.

Two months ago I celebrated my 31st birthday. Maman et papa were so happy over the phone. Élodie baked me a cake. We had a party. All our friends were there. Elarif got wasted and kept on telling me how much I look like you. I had a great time. I always do when there's noise around me. But then everybody left and Élodie went to sleep. I couldn't because the apartment was a mess or maybe because I was a year older than you will ever be. So I started cleaning up. The next morning, she found me sitting on the couch and she knew as she always did. But she didn't make a sound. That's how I knew I was in trouble. That's why I wanted to get away for Christmas. That's how we ended up in Luxembourg. It's probably the worst idea I've ever had.

I stared out a window today. Don't worry, I wasn't going to jump. I mean if I had to pick, going out a window wouldn't be my choice. I am still terrified of heights. I don't know how you did it. Anyway, I just wanted to tell you about Élodie. It was about time you met or maybe a bit too late. We were supposed to go to one of her friends for New Year's Eve, but now I'll be going to Elarif's, probably. I see why you two were such good friends. He's always up to something and he always has a funny story to tell. Maybe she'll come too. I've been calling her every morning since we came back. She hasn't picked up yet. I don't know what I'll say if she does. But she will eventually because half her things are here. I don't want to give them back and I don't want to let her go. But maybe she is right. Maybe, I don't know how to live any other way. I don't even know how to try. Maybe, I'll just tell her that I'm sorry and that I tried to try. I'll tell her that I love her because I do. I don't think she'll believe me, but I'll tell her anyway.

Tu me manques et je t'embrasse

Guillaume

WEEGIE BOARD
Drew Taylor

Detective Sole arrived at the crime scene knowing it was his last chance. The superintendent had made this clear, both of them surprised that someone was still interested in Sole's services.

He ducked under the police tape and rolled his suitcase into the derelict flat where he met Inspector Close and her two officers in the unfurnished living room.

'Sole?' she asked, puffing her cigarette.

He wheezed a confirmation, having lugged his suitcase up ten flights thanks to the lift's 'Out of Order' sign.

She led him into the bedroom, also cordoned off with tape. Rubbish, mainly old newspapers, covered most of its bare floorboards, while the flowery wallpaper was torn and enhanced by crude graffiti. In the middle lay the victim face down in his own blood.

'Danny McManus, aged 21,' Close said, leaning against the doorframe. 'Multiple stab wounds to the chest. No murder weapon, no witnesses. Considering his age and the area, you're looking at a standard Glasgow gangland killing.'

Sole looked at the body. His first case had been the fourth victim of a notorious serial killer. He'd needed an escort to guide him through the mob of journalists just to get to the crime scene, everyone hopeful he'd crack the case. They hadn't called when they'd found the fifth victim.

'How long since...?' he asked, laying his suitcase flat.

'Forensics estimates six hours.'

Sole nodded. The earliest he'd ever got to a body was twelve hours.

'They've got everything?' he asked. 'Place might get a bit messy.'

'The room is yours.' She smiled and trickled smoke from between her teeth and out her nostrils. 'I just wanted to see you in action.'

'I'm afraid I'll need complete privacy.'

Close eyed Sole. 'Look, you know no one gives a shit about this kid. I heard you were on your last legs and thought I might as well call you out and see if you do something. I mean, you obviously think you can.'

Sole tried to turn his wince into a smile. 'I'm flattered. But it won't work with you in the room.'

She let out a guttural sigh. 'Like it's worked already.' She flicked her cigarette butt into the room and walked off, muttering that she'd never help anyone again. He closed the door behind her. It didn't have a lock, but the latch clicked shut. He stared at its faded and chipped wooden surface and thought about leaving, accepting his fate. But when he looked at what was Danny McManus he knew he had to stay.

He threw on his robe with the detective's badge on the chest and folded out his knee-high table, placing his board and sand timer on top. Hood up, he encircled the body in a ring of ash, this time including the table within it, which he'd never done before. Lit candles were placed at the feet, shoulders, and head, and he opened his small birdcage to release his white dove and black nightjar into the room.

Kneeling at the table, Sole heard the muffled laughs of Close and the officers through the wall, and he tried to ignore the voice in his head that said he was about to commit his third and final failure. He looked at the body, exhaled, and turned the sand timer over, placing his hands in the board's grooves.

Eyes closed, he started his chant: 'In darkness I can see, bring this lost one back to me.'

For a while nothing happened, and the voice in his head confirmed its doubts. But Sole soon realised that the birds were flying above him anticlockwise over the ring of ash, equidistant from each other. That hadn't happened before.

He continued his chant and soon felt breeze on his face. He heard the papers rustle and small shards skitter along the floorboards. It built into a surging wind that whipped all the paper and rubbish into a swirl that stayed outside the ring of ash.

A light flashed so brightly Sole saw it beneath his eyelids. He opened them to see a dot of light above the body. He stopped and stuttered for the next phrase. He'd never got this far before. But before the dot could fade and the wind could die, he remembered:

'Into the light! Into the light!'

The dot expanded into a green-tinged orb and crackled branches of silent lightning.

And then he heard it:

HELL… ACHING…

He chanted faster and louder, tears running from his eyes. The orb cracked and flooded the room in white light, and Sole shielded his eyes with his hands. The light faded, leaving Sole in the centre of the silent swirl of papers.

AH SAID, DAE AH SMELL BACON?

Sole lowered his hands to see the glowing white and diaphanous shape of Danny McManus hovering in the air like a life-sized pencil sketch.

Sole froze – he'd done it, he'd finally done it. His amazement blocked all of his senses, and he failed to register Danny's attempt to communicate, or Danny's realisation that his own hands were transparent, and that he was hovering over his bloodied corpse.

THE FUCK? W-W-WHUT IS THIS?

Sole snapped back. He'd scripted a delicate piece to keep the spirit calm. But, his mind still mushy, he blurted out, 'Danny, you're dead. Calm down.'

Danny frowned.

DEED? WHUT THE FUCK? AM NO DEED AM...

His face fell.

AW NAW. AH REMEMBUR. IT'S TRUE. AM...

Danny screamed and tried to fly off, but he couldn't pass the ash, so he pinged back and forth, around and around unable to escape, bawling his head off.

Sole glanced at the timer and saw he had little time. He shouted for Danny to stop, but the ghost kept screaming and flying. Eventually, after shouting several more times, Sole got Danny's attention. Danny's lips quivered and his eyes looked to be filling with tears.

'Listen – I'm a police officer and I brought you back so you can tell us who did this to you. Tell me and I'll ensure we get a conviction.' Sole made a fist.

Danny's fear twisted into a grimace.

FUCK AFF. AM NO TELLIN YOU ANYTHIN.

Sole blinked. 'Danny, I'm serious. You can't mess around here.'

AM NO GRASS.

Only a few morsels of sand remained in the timer. Sole cursed his sloppiness.

'Danny, in a few seconds you're going to be gone forever. If you don't tell me who did this then they might get away with it.'

AW RIGHT. WELL, IT WAS YER MAW. AYE, SHE POISONED MA SANNY AFTER AH FUCKED HER.

Danny thrusted his crotch and grunted. The last of the sand trickled away and his chest sliced open, flooding the room in light. He raised his arms and sang:

IF YE WANNA GO TAE HEAVEN WHEN YE DIE,

THEN YE GOTTA WEAR A THISTLE SCARF AND THISTLE TIE!

Sole shielded his eyes and Danny's voice died away. The light disappeared and Sole lowered his hands to see the papers fluttering back to the floor and the birds resting in opposite corners.

He stayed on his knees and gazed at where the ghost had been – the ghost that he had summoned.

The bedroom door crashed open, followed by Close and the two officers. Heaving deeply, she looked around at the reorganised mess.

'What happened? Did you lock the door?'

'T-the door?'

'You didn't hear us banging?'

'No, no,' Sole said, rising to his feet. 'I did it. I summoned him.'

Close blinked. 'You what?'

'Oh ho!' one of the officers shouted. He clapped his hands and held them out to Close and the other officer. 'Pay up.'

Close folded her arms and eyed Sole. 'So who did it then?'

'Hmm?'

'Who killed Danny McManus?'

'Oh, well, he wouldn't actually say…'

A smile tweezed out Close's lips, and the triumphant officer dropped his head.

'So you summoned him but he didn't talk?' she said, adding a laugh.

45

'He didn't –'

'He didn't summon anything,' Close said, shaking her head to the officers. 'He can't admit that he can't do it. The superintendent's going to hear all about this.'

They walked out, Close on her phone, leaving Sole to tidy up. He paid them no bother. He knew what he'd accomplished.

He was folding his robe when his phone rang. The superintendent's number.

'We're suspending your services indefinitely,' he said. 'Report to the reception desk tomorrow morning. And I'll need your detective's badge.'

'Sir, if I could –'

'I don't want to hear it. I shouldn't have ever listened to you about this magical shit.' The line clicked.

Sole slid his phone back into his pocket. The birds chirped and sunlight shone through the window, glinting the detective's badge against the black of the robe.

Sole smiled, unclipped the badge, and placed it inside the ring of ash. Suitcase packed, he rolled it out of the flat and started the descent down the ten flights of stairs, thinking of names for his new PI company.

CLOUDS

Michael Worrell

The weather forecast said it was going to be sunny and clear on the day of the fair, and for the most part it was. I only saw two small clouds throughout the day, and neither of them lasted long. I noticed the first one while I was in line at a stall selling conch fritters. I'd been distracted by the storyteller and dance show, so I was already late getting home to Jasmine, but I'd come here with a purpose and I wasn't going to give her my praise of a folktale performance when she'd sent me out for fritters.

The line wasn't long, but the food stalls were packed so close together in their little corner of the fair that there wasn't much space to separate those wandering about and those waiting to purchase. I shoved my hands in my pockets to ward off pickpockets. There were enough moving bodies that someone could easily be caught unawares and never know who'd done it. But with my fingers over my valuables, anyone who saw me would know I was no easy mark.

Unfortunately, that meant I didn't have those hands readily

available when I was taken. My arm and shoulder were grabbed from behind, and I was pulled out of line. I only had time to exclaim 'Wha-' as I was spun around and pulled into a kiss. My mind was racing. It couldn't be Jasmine, she'd stayed home and we only had one car. My exes both hated me, so it couldn't be any of them. Hot air rushed into my lungs as I pushed myself away. I felt myself begin to sweat. Was this assault? I reeled back, my hands flailing out of my pockets, and as I did, the stranger stumbled away as well.

That was when I saw the first cloud. It was black, not tarnished silver like a rain cloud or the angry grey of a storm, just black, like swirling smoke. It hovered above us, and as I regained my balance, a flash of light seared the air around me. Static crackled in my nostrils. The man - as I could now see it had been a man - lay on the ground in a charred blackened heap. I smelled barbecue. How wrong was it, I wondered, to find the smell of someone struck by lightning appetizing? Was that a damning offence?

'Ooh. I don't know. Probably.'

I was surprised when I heard the voice, not because I didn't recognize it, but because I didn't expect it. I hadn't said anything out loud. I turned my head to find who had spoken and felt a wave of dizziness instead. I hadn't moved. I was still staring at the burnt, silent corpse in front of me. Without my telling it to, I felt my head lean upwards to look at the cloud, which I now saw was rapidly dispersing.

'That's not good,' said the same unfamiliar voice.

I was feeling dizzy at this point. 'What's going on?'

'Oh, sorry. I'm Nathan. Nice to meet you, sorry about the circumstances.' Now I was turning around, and I saw the crowd of people around me beginning to break out of stunned silence into panicked flight. I felt my legs begin pumping, and it took me a moment after the world began bouncing to realize I was running as well. It was like watching the world through the lens of a shaky camera while my body was being piloted on strings. Like one of those creepy dolls.

'A marionette, you mean?' asked Nathan.

'You're in my head?'

'Not exactly *in* your head. Think of it as sharing. Won't be for very long, mind. I just need to borrow you for a minute, and then we can go our separate ways and this body will be completely under the control of... uh...'

'My name's Andrew,' I said. We had stopped running. The panic hadn't lasted long, just enough for the nearby crowd to crash into the crowds further back and remember that lightning never strikes twice in the same place. A kind of haphazard perimeter had formed around the scorched probably-corpse. A few began sheepishly running forward to see if he was dead. Why couldn't I hear anything?

'Completely under the control of Andrew!' Nathan finished. 'Thank you. You can't hear anything because everyone's screaming right now and if I let that through, you wouldn't be able to hear me at all. Now, you haven't seen anyone wearing a pinstripe suit at the fair, have you? Dark eyes, talking on a phone, holding a thin metal stick? Like a... wand, let's say?'

I ran through the hour since I had arrived at the fairgrounds. 'Um, no. Not that I can remember.'

'That's fine.' I was tiptoeing now, my head craning up, looking over the crowd. 'Can't be far. Dropping a bolt like that is a pretty close thing. Keep an eye out – erm...mind out.'

I didn't like the idea that something like that could happen again. Something in me wanted to shiver. As it was, I merely felt an odd sense of emptiness where I suppose my spine should have been.

'Don't worry. I've been doing this a long time. As long as we find them first, there won't be a problem.' He sounded more confident than I wanted to credit.

'I have a wife.'

'My sympathies. I hope you won't be in trouble for being kissed by a stran-' We both saw a man wearing a pinstriped suit step towards the blackened man on the ground at the same time and chorused, 'There he is!'

'What now?' I thought.

Nathan sounded thoughtful. 'That depends. Have you ever been in a fight?'

'What? No!' I waved my hands in front of me, or I would have, if I'd been able. Instead, I was struck by a bout of dizziness as my mind reached for something that wasn't there anymore.

'Athletic? Do you play sports?' He was moving us along the perimeter, slowly angling us closer to Pinstripes' backside. I hoped he was planning to run and not jump this guy.

'I used to play tennis, but the last time was two years ago. Why?' The last thing I needed was to have to explain to Jasmine why I was arrested for assault after I got my body back.

'Just a thought, oh!' A girl in sweats stood next to us. Nathan had her centre frame in our vision. 'She looks fit.'

I'd seen her on stage during the storyteller's show. Of course, she hadn't been in sweats then. She'd been in costume, dancing in the role of the Chickcharney, a huge bird that bestowed luck, good or ill, upon those it met. There had been a lot of jumping involved to mimic flight, and I had envied how fit she was. I had never been in that kind of shape, and I probably never would.

'Dancers are perfect! Thank you Andrew. I hope you enjoy the rest of your life. If I can time this right, then I should be able to -' he swiveled our head back to look at Pinstripes, who was still talking on the phone, but almost immediately locked eyes with us. He raised his other hand, and in it I saw what looked like a metal wand pointing directly at me.

'What's that?' I asked.

'Nevermindherewego.' Nathan grabbed the girl and I felt my body and lips press into hers as a warm breeze blew out of my lungs. For the first time I realized I hadn't breathed at all since Nathan had taken over. My body came back to me like a car slamming going at 60 mph. I fell away, onto my rump, the sounds of the fairground roaring to fill the silence Nathan had imposed. I sucked in air greedily.

That was when I saw the second cloud, black and pregnant, directly above me.

THE WEEKEND GETAWAY

Elena Sturk Lussier

The cottage is level with the lake. During storms, the waves glide on the sand and lap at the foundation. Now, the water is still. The maples and oaks around the cottage have turned red and yellow. The sky is grey and overcast and the line between the lake and the sky has melted into uniformity. In the distance, along the beach, a lone fire emits a stream of smoke.

They are in the sunroom at the front of the cottage.

'It's your turn, honey,' she says.

She rubs her hands together and tucks them under her armpits; she never tires of the feel of a good cashmere sweater. They have turned on the radiators but it'll be hours before the place is heated.

The man is looking at the lake and its stillness. 'Christ, where did summer go?'

They are sitting in and surrounded by relics: two wicker chairs around an oak table; a brown carpet dented by furniture feet;

a basket filled with old woollen blankets and shawls; a floral-patterned velvet sofa.

'I put down *happy*,' she says.

The man looks down at the board.

'How many points was that?' he asks.

'Twelve.'

'Well, I've got shit all so it might take me a while.'

'That's all right, I'll put the kettle on.'

She gets up from the wicker chair, its strained strands creaking under her, and walks to the kitchen. She has a thick pair of woollen socks on her feet from their last trip to Cape Cod, but her toes are still frozen.

'You want some?' she calls from the kitchen.

'Hm?'

'Would you like some tea?'

'Is there Earl Grey?'

She rummages through the cabinet.

'Sure is,' she says.

'All right, then.'

She fills the kettle with water and puts it on the stove and comes back to her wicker chair. He's hunched over in his own chair, his fists under his chin, his thick brows furrowed. Even when he wears a sweater, she can see his leanness, his sharpness, the hours he puts in the gym. He still has a full head of hair, for which she's thankful. He looks young, she thinks. He runs his fingers through his greying hair and the gold Rolex on his wrist glints.

'Have you put anything down yet?' she asks.

He's staring at his letters as if he's hoping to find one he hasn't noticed before.

'I hate this game,' he says. 'Always makes me feel stupid. You'd think I'd be good at it.'

'You teach History, not English.'

'Same difference.'

'Just put anything down; I'm sure you've got something.'

He rises and she brings him down, over and over, like a dance, as if he were a helium balloon and she the hand of a small child.

'Sure, I can put a few things down, but they don't make up more than four points. How am I supposed to win like that?'

The kettle whistles. She goes to the kitchen, puts two tea bags in the pot and pours the boiling water over them, feeling the steam tickle her nostrils.

'You know?' he calls from the sunroom. 'I don't know what I'm drinking tea for. It's four o'clock. Bring me a Scotch, will you?'

She takes two mugs from the shelf. Above the fridge, there's three quarters of a bottle of Scotch left. She drops two ice cubes in one of the mugs, pours two fingers – no, three – and brings the teapot and the mugs to the table, dropping a placemat under the teapot to protect the oak from the heat of the ceramic.

She sits and looks at the board. Still no progress.

'Well, do you want to play something else? Cribbage?' she asks.

He scoffs, leans back in his chair. 'Cribbage? Christ, you talk as if we're elderly.'

She smiles without warmth. 'Well, we're nearly there.'

'No. We're not.'

'Whatever you say, honey.'

He gets up from his chair and starts pacing the length of the sunroom. His arms are crossed and one hand is caressing his chin. She imagines he does the same when he teaches. The floorboards creak under his every step.

She takes the pot and pours hot tea into her mug, then takes the mug into her hands, trying to warm them, and softly blows on the tea.

'Have some Scotch,' she says, but doesn't move to pass him the mug; he pauses in his pacing, walks over and reaches to take the handle – he knows it's more of a command than a suggestion.

'We should bring proper glasses with us next time,' he comments, looking down at his mug.

A hummingbird flits in front of the windows, surely its last appearance before winter, and guzzles for a moment at the birdfeeder.

He drinks his Scotch and she sips her tea.

'I haven't changed my mind,' she says.

He says nothing.

'He had a joint,' she says, as if it explains everything.

She crosses her legs, trying to make herself small, trying to keep her core warm.

'Hell, maybe Martha's right, maybe it was just one joint,' his voice strained, hopeful.

'That's how these things start.'

He looks out the window; she can only see his profile.

'Can't we just put him in a different school?' he asks.

'Military school *is* a different school.'

'And what message is that going to send?'

She can see the white of his knuckles gripping the handle of his mug.

He continues: 'We have one kid and we can't even manage to raise him well, set him straight?'

The wind outside is picking up a little. Tiny waves lap at the beach, one over the other, taking over, interrupting the other's stride.

'Military school *will* set him straight.'

His jaw clenches. 'Christ, I can't believe we've arrived at *military school* as our only option. I'm not convinced we've tried everything yet.'

'*I have* tried everything.'

Her voice is sharp, immediate; it seems to cut through the buzz of questions inside his head; he turns around to look at her, finally. She meets his gaze and doesn't blink; he's the first to look away.

'What do we know about this place?' he asks, more softly now. 'Apart from that it's going to cost us a fortune.'

She sips her tea. 'You remember Alan, our CFO? He sent his kid there. Straightened him right out.'

He sighs, puts a hand in his pocket. 'What are we going to tell people?'

She shrugs. 'We'll say he's studying abroad.'

He lets out a humourless chuckle. 'You've really thought this through, haven't you?'

She looks out at the grey lake and the grey sky and wonders if it's going to rain. He looks out the window with her. The hummingbird is gone.

'Can we try to relax a little?' she asks.

He looks at her and gives a tired smile. She looks at the grey hairs at his temples and resists the urge to touch her own. Together for better, for worse.

He finishes his Scotch, comes towards her to set down his mug on the table, then goes to the sofa. He lies down, an arm behind his head, and closes his eyes. 'I'm exhausted.'

She is too, but she would never admit it to him or to herself. 'You sleep, now, honey,' she says. 'This weekend is for us. When you wake up, I'll make you a nice steak.'

The wind is blowing harder. It whistles through cracks in the windows.

'This place is falling apart,' he mutters from the sofa. 'We should get our own cottage.'

'Maybe next year,' she says.

She pours herself more tea and holds the mug under her face

so she can feel the steam on her skin. After a few minutes, she still hasn't warmed up, so she gets up and takes two blankets from the wicker basket. She lays one blanket across her husband, looks at the lines around his eyes, then bends down to kiss his forehead.

'Imagine how relaxed we'll be once he's gone,' she says.

He opens his eyes. 'Then it'll be just the two of us, like back in the day.'

She smiles. 'Maybe you could take me out, once in a while.'

He laughs; a low rumble. She leaves him to sit down in her chair, tucking the blanket under her chin and wrapping it around her legs. She closes her eyes. Maybe now she'll get warm.

BLAME IT ON THE WIND

Mark Holmes

I was already thirty years old when I'd had to move back home to live with my mother.

It was a Wednesday morning, a month or so after, and we were sat on opposite sofas in the front room wearing our dressing gowns and eating our breakfasts. I was eating croissants with butter and jam, sweet black coffee, and a sliced orange. I would sip the coffee then suck on a slice of the orange and it tasted good. My mother had a bowl of Cinnamon Shreddies and a mug of tea with milk and two sugars.

'Pretty good,' I said.

'Ssshhh,' she said, 'Popmaster is on.'

She turned the radio up.

'Doesn't Kate Bush sound like Björk?' I said, 'or, rather, Björk sounds like Kate Bush.'

'No she doesn't.'

'I bet I could play you between five and ten Björk songs that sound just like this. She certainly cites her as an influence. I read it somewhere. In MOJO magazine. PJ Harvey does too.'

'I don't think so,' said my mother.

'How much Björk do you listen to?'

'Let's agree to disagree,' said my mother.

✻

'He seems nice,' I said, referring to the contestant on the radio.

'Why don't you marry him then?' she said.

The dog came in and my mother pulled him up onto the sofa beside her.

'Who's a gorgeous one?' she said to him, moving his paws up and down in her hands. 'You're a gorgeous one, aren't you?' she said.

I didn't hear who won the quiz.

✻

'There was a bloke at the bus stop yesterday,' I said, finishing my coffee, 'I was stood in the way of the bus timetable and guess what he did...' My mother wasn't listening. 'Never mind,' I said.

'Go on...' she said, 'you were at the bus stop...'

'It doesn't matter,' I said, 'it's not important.'

I took my dirty dishes into the kitchen, rinsed them under the tap and placed them in the dishwasher. My mother followed me.

'What's up with you?' she said.

'Nothing, I'm fine,' I said, 'I'm going in the shower.'

'Jesus Christ,' she said, under her breath.

I walked upstairs to the bathroom, locked the door, pulled off my pyjamas, flicked the radio on and sat down on the toilet. There was no sound from the radio so I had to shit in silence. Once I was finished and flushed I fiddled with the volume control but there was still nothing. Then I saw that the plug from the radio was wrapped around its underneath.

'Jesus Christ,' I said and wrapped a towel around myself. I took the lead by the plug end and stretched it under the bathroom door, then under the bedroom door next to the bathroom and into the plug socket on the bedroom wall. The radio burst into life.

'Next up is tracks of my years...' said Ken Bruce.

I got back into the bathroom and locked the door, turned the shower on and got in. Mark Billingham had picked 'Life is a Rollercoaster' by Ronan Keating as one of his tracks of his years. I sang along and adjusted the temperature on the shower. There was a knock at the bathroom door.

'Are you still in there?!' my mother shouted, 'I need a poo!'

'Hang on! Can you wait?' I replied.

'What?!' she shouted back, 'I can't hear you, the radio is too loud.'

'HANG ON!' I shouted, 'CAN YOU WAIT!?'

'No!' she replied, 'I'm desperate.'

'Hang on then,' I shouted.

'What!?' she shouted back.

'HANG ON!'

'I can't hang on, I'm desperate!'

'No, I mean 'Hang on, I'm getting out!' Hang on a minute!'

I left the shower running and got out, wrapped the towel around me and unlocked the door. My mother pushed past me and shoved me out of the bathroom.

'Hurry up! I'm desperate!' she said.

She locked the door behind her and turned the shower and

the radio off. I shivered in the hallway as the carpet soaked up the water from my feet. Salt water ran down my forehead and into my right eye, stinging so badly that I had to keep it closed. I could hear my mother shitting. A splash followed by a frantic gathering of toilet roll followed by the sound of wiping. Like a finger running down the page of a book. I heard a flush and the washing of hands as she sang the theme to Popmaster in a robotic voice.

'POP-MAS-TER!' she said as she unlocked the door, doing a robotic break-dance move with her arms. The smell hit me immediately. It smelt like the meat raffle at an egg-festival. I retched.

'There you go, Old Grumpy Grandpa,' she said.

I ignored her and walked back into the bathroom and locked the door.

'Did you hear what I called you?' she shouted after me.

'No, what?' I shouted back.

'Old Grumpy Grandpa!' she shouted, 'You're an Old Grumpy Grandpa!'

'No, I'm not!' I shouted back.

I opened all the windows and sprayed some room freshener that I found in the bathroom cabinet and I turned the radio back on and got in the shower. It was freezing cold from the toilet being flushed. Then suddenly scalding hot. Then freezing cold again.

'Fuck! Jesus!' I shouted, as I leapt away from the stream of water, knocking bottles of shampoo and shower gel and face wash all over the bottom of the bathtub. I heard my mother shouting and swearing and slamming her bedroom door as I picked up the bottles and rearranged them on the side of the bath. Then I heard the front door slam and I knew that later she would blame that on the wind. I peered out of the bathroom window and watched her drive away with the dog. I looked at my hands and I moved my thumb over the tan-line where my wedding band had been.

'Jesus fucking Christ,' I said to myself.

Bahaa' (Glory)
(from an upcoming short-story collection titled *Tales of a Tour Guide*)

Ronnie Chatah

27 December 2013

An armed security guard positioned himself by a door dividing the emergency room from a cordoned off corridor. My final moment to reconsider.

My vision was blurred from tears, and my throat sore from screams. Toufic had driven me there. A family friend for many years, he had arrived the moment he knew. Photojournalists and television crews waited at the hospital's entrance. He did his best to speak on my behalf and keep them at bay. This was nothing new for a city used to such events. People knocking on my door, my car window, approaching me anywhere I went. Offering condolences when I walked on Beirut's *corniche* or when I trekked remote villages of Mount Lebanon. Any attempt at being alone was drowned in a flood of sympathy. I had inherited celebrity status - not of famed acclaim, but of sorrow and pity. Political assassinations afford such luxury in Lebanon. They hugged me and expressed their love for my dad, wanting to share their opinions of *al waðaã* - the situation. My loss was tied to the region's politics and war, and I navigated those subjects as best as I could. In the weeks after his murder, an internal silence, a necessary detachment, kept my true emotions from showing. If anything, all the attention helped create a facade, a false reality. The cameras, the microphones. Mourning took time.

That morning, I was shielded enough from public view. And it was my decision. Mine alone.

'Daroure ɗhufu.'

The guard made brief eye contact with me, before lowering his gaze and quietly uttering the phrase I would hear a thousand times over:

'Allah yehfazou.'

The door opened to a dimly lit hallway under repair. Neon lights dangled below electrical wires, exposing the ceiling's inner workings. The American University Hospital. An institution under renovation, built in the 1950s as an extension to the American University of Beirut. Staying open throughout Lebanon's civil war, repeated Israeli invasions, Syrian occupation. In recent years, the casualties of car bombings.

A nurse ushered me through, her surgical mask hindering unnecessary words. She braced my arm. Other staff stood against lime-green coloured walls as we passed, whispering affirmations that I was his son. The glossy floor squeaked with each step, my hastily donned shoes treading over neon reflections on the adhesive tiles.

We reached another security guard who asked us to wait. *'Fatu jemeãa min al mahkameh'* - Tribunal investigators inside. The Special Tribunal for Lebanon, which my father helped establish following the assassination of his former boss, prime minister Rafik Hariri. The Tribunal's purpose: to uncover the criminals responsible, and prevent further assassinations from taking place. The Tribunal had accused members of Hezbollah. And Hezbollah had retaliated.

A doctor emerged. He told the security guard the investigators had left. The deep bags under his eyes spoke to an exhausting double-shift, his scruff needed shaving. He slowly placed a hand on my shoulder, and took a deep breath. But before he spoke, I knew. A car bombing in downtown Beirut that tore apart the facades of nearby buildings, leaving a two-metre crater in the pavement. The echo of that explosion reaching my apartment across the city, killing and injuring multiple passersby. I had seen the news, and dropped my phone to my father's name: Mohamad Bahaa' Chatah.

'I know you want to do this,' the doctor began with a calm, measured voice. 'And it is your right to see him.'

His pager went off. I looked past him, towards the end of the corridor. A final door.

'But I don't think,' the pager interrupted again, he switched it off. 'I don't think you should. I've seen what this does. You will only hurt more.'

His advice made no difference. I could only look beyond that final door. And the only words I spoke that morning, rang true once more.

'Daroure shufu.'

The room was brightly lit. Surgeons in white operating gowns stood behind the operating table. They looked above me. Trying, with simple gesture to offer me a few seconds of being unobserved. My father lay between us.

His face, torn away. Scalp burned to dark red, feeding to charcoal black. His head resting on its side, cracked. A body bag wrapped around his chest. From its shape, I could tell...his arms, his legs, now belonged to the wreckage. The casing zipped low enough, to expose his graying chest hair.

Without tears. Without breaking down. In that room, it all

pulsed through me.

Swimming in a nearby pool as he dips below the surface and lifts me to his shoulders, tossing me up, splashing back down to the water. I swim back towards him, and see his chest. He lifts me once more, and keeps me on his shoulders. I look below to the water, my ankles rubbing against him.

Holding onto the steering wheel...he takes me for a ride. Sweltering heat and no air conditioning. We're shirtless, and my back is against his itchy chest. He's letting me 'drive'. I'm in his lap, we're on an empty road. He controls the foot pedals and hands me control, at the slowest of speeds.

Reflecting in the mirror. My body is changing, overnight. He stands next to me. We're the same height. In bath robes, our chests exposed. Shaving cream shared. My third attempt, his daily routine. Aware of what awaits, unaware of our glory.

The body bag was slowly sealed shut. The only emotion I expressed that morning was when they took him away. I pulled at my own chest hair. I let it tear.

I left the hospital to flashbulbs and questions. Toufic rushed me to his car and we drove away. When I reached my mom, our relatives, friends, and neighbours were at her side. My family home quickly became the public's domain. By that afternoon, hundreds had gathered. The interviews began that evening.

Two days later, I bid him farewell. To the chants of Martyrs Square, and to the tragedy of Lebanon circumstances. Now I was turning around, and I saw the crowd of people around me beginning to break out of stunned silence into panicked flight.

LOVESEAT

Raymond Vermeulen

It all started with the loveseat. A bright, garish shade of pink, it was the perfect complement to the ivory coffee table pointed at the 52" flat screen television. Bob was an interior designer. At least, that's how he chose to spend most of his time. The truth is, Bob was never really short of money. Being free of financial concerns, Bob could afford to indulge whatever whims took his fancy. And right now that was building his dream house. Picking out the exact shade of cream needed to brighten up a room, coordinating household appliances with luxuriously over-the-top lampshades, building the greatest media center known to man... Bob hadn't yet realized that without earning any of it, he'd soon grow bored and move on to other ways of entertaining himself — but none of that mattered at the moment. For now, the designer in him really wanted that loveseat. It would make for a perfectly tasteful arrangement, truly a room to die in. But it all rang rather hollow.

The fact is that Bob was lonely. Not needing to work meant he spent most of his time cooped up inside, which isn't the greatest way to meet women. Sure, sometimes the neighbours would wander by and make light conversation, the occasional cute pizza delivery girl showed up, but he never really made a move. Whether he'd admit it or not, Bob was painfully shy. He could have anything money could buy, except for a date.

The loveseat was an unexpected wakeup call. What was the point of owning a loveseat, of owning the perfect house, without having anyone to share it with? He could spend days swimming in his private pool or cooking 5 star meals in his fully equipped kitchen, but this would all just serve to highlight his lonely existence. So he decided on his next project. He'd stop messing around with furniture and concentrate on the final step of building his dream house. He'd turn this bachelor pad into a family home.

Soon, Bob was joined by a short, slender redhead who strolled up to his front gate. A warm smile was painted on her face and her voice dripped with pure seduction. They wasted little time.

'Ah, van vesua! Cummuns nala,' she beamed. 'Za woka genava.'

'Gwanda blitz.' Bob nodded.

'Elicanto...' she sighed.

Leaving the lovers to their embrace, Bob hit F5, saving his Sim household. Taking a sip of his Dr. Pepper as he once again opened up the designer interface, he was quite pleased with himself. Now he could finally justify buying Bob that loveseat.

THE FIREWORKS ON
CROMER PIER
Drew Townsend

The morning sunshine spilled into the Field Marshal's office. As it did, it illuminated the likeness of King George V above the mantelpiece in such a way that the occupant became momentarily distracted from the field report he inspected. It was during this momentary distraction that the Field Marshal's clerk knocked at the door, and on being permitted entry, asked for a moment of his employer's time.

'A letter has arrived, sir. It was recovered from the body of Officer Jack Hopkins of the 54th East Anglian Division. It's an unusual letter, sir, hence why it's reached you.'

The Field Marshal took the letter and briefly inspected its muddied state. Then he held it under the morning light, where he read each scrawled word carefully:

Gallipoli, ~~24~~ᵗʰ August 1915

Dear Millie,

~~This night was the third~~ *Last night was the third time I've attacked the enemy line. I was hit and badly wounded in the hip. I have been here a while. I don't think anyone is coming for me. I have tried to move, but it is impossible. ~~I think I will~~ Not a back to blighty one I guess. Do not worry that I am in pain or discomfort. My hip is quite numb, and I feel strangely at peace. I think I must be lying somewhere nearer the enemy lines than our own. The attack was supposed to draw out the enemy counter offensive, but all we drew was their machine gun fire. We attacked at night and now it is night again. I think it is the 24ᵗʰ but I'm not sure. Fortunately, I filled my lighter before the attack as I now write under its light. I almost forgot I had pen and paper. I reached for my cigarettes and found them in the same pocket.*

I hope my men are ok. When I heard the machine guns open up I told my men to hold, while I advanced to see what was happening. I saw the first advance had all perished, and then I was hit. Hopefully the retreat was sounded and my men are safe. Our attack must have been a failure, but we did our duty with the courage the King demands and this soothes me. My father can be proud.

I will write to my mother after this letter, but if I do not survive long enough, please tell her I love her, or if this is too much of a burden to bear then, if by some miracle this letter makes it to you, please show her so she can know that I thought of her in my final hours, and my brother Tom, who I hope comes of age too late to follow in my footsteps, and father too, who I hope is well and not too troubled by the constant news of loss he must have to hear at the parish meetings.

The reason I write to you, Millie, as perhaps you already know, I'm not sure - is that I love you so very deeply. I know that I have never said so, that perhaps to you I was just the boy who teased you when we played in the meadow or stole your dolls at Tina Collison's birthday party, but I love you, Millie, more than any girl I ever knew. I have loved you ever since we were nine. Perhaps I did not know it quite as I do now. I always thought you would remain in my life, you were the one constant throughout my childhood.

Suddenly I feel quite cold.

~~Sorry~~

~~I wanted~~ I had wished to go to your eighteenth birthday party at the town hall, and I had planned on telling you all this then, but alas I was fast tracked to basic training. The Turks giving us too much hell. Just before we shipped, I thought about coming to your house, but in all honesty, I was afraid you might reject me, and I didn't want to go to Gallipoli knowing that you did not love me.

I resolved that when I came back I would pluck up the courage to ask you for a day of your time. The whole time over here I've been thinking of where I would take you and what we would do.

My plan was to go to the Fireworks at Comer Pier on the 5th of November, but I thought we'd make a journey of it. We could get the train to Kings Lynn where we could go to the café in the Tuesday market place. I hear from Thomas that you and Jeanie Smith go there frequently, how is she? I heard her brother died at ~~Gallipoli~~ Flanders., I didn't know him very well, but he seemed a decent Officer and a good fellow.

At the cafe, we would have a breakfast of sausage and eggs or just French toast if you weren't too hungry. If their coffee was good - I know you like your coffee - then we could perk ourselves up before getting the bus to Sandringham where we could walk the forest trail and perhaps catch sight of a deer or two. I seem to remember there being a rather lovely little tea room there that serves cream scones with generous helpings of jam. If you were not too full of toast or sausages, then perhaps we could indulge a little, bear in mind this is my treat, not a penny would be spared on your part.

~~Then we will~~ Then we would get the train from Lynn to Cromer. Have you been to the fireworks there? I went as a small child, and I remember it was the most wonderful thing I had ever seen. Often as the artillery barrages have thundered overhead, causing me to take refuge in my trench, I've imagined I was standing on Cromer Pier on the 5th of November, the Ferris wheels spinning, the rockets whirling in the air, hot cocoa in my hand, marshmallows melting and sweetening the bitterness of the chocolate. *I think you would love it, Millie. The way the smell of the fireworks lingers in the air, the way the waves slosh underneath the pier, the sweet remembrance of childhood, innocence, happiness. Would all this help you realise I love you? Would we look up at the sparks raining down all around us and imagine our life together? A house in the village just down from the cricket pavilion, one of the little ones with the thatched roofs. ~~Would we see our children?~~ Would we see our children? A boy, a girl, more if you wanted or none at all. Perhaps I've had too long to think about all this, but I just want you to know that I love you, Millie.*

Perhaps I am a coward telling you all this with the knowledge that I will never hear your response, never tell you face to face. Perhaps this letter will be crushed into the dirt of the battlefield or burnt along with my uniform once the enemy has stripped me of my possessions. Or the wind will carry it across the Aegean to a poet who can convey my love for you far better than I. But if you do get this letter, Millie, I want you to do in life whatever makes you happy, and think of me maybe. Perhaps go see the fireworks on Cromer pier, and have a cocoa for me.

Yours ~~lovingly~~

eternally,

Jack

The Field Marshal finished reading, and stared silently at the mud stained letter.

'Well, sir?'

'We can't send this, type a telegram saying the usual, he died without suffering, signed by the chaplain.'

'But the girl, sir...'

'We can't make exceptions, send a telegram, I'll hear no more of this. This should never have come to me.'

And with that, the clerk was dismissed. The Field Marshal sat back down at his desk and looked up briefly at the likeness of King George again, before turning his attention back to his field report.

HEROINE
Yanting Zhang

I am a fire afar off,
a sword laid aside.

> By Miguel de Cervantes Saavedra, *Don Quixote*

Amy is sitting alone in the dining hall, looking at her macaroni and lemonade. Avoiding possible eye contact with others, she barely lifts her eyelids. I know she is ashamed, because nobody wants to sit by her, at least not now.

I am facing straight towards her from two tables across, and I can see the tortured look on her face: the color of her cheek is pale and sickly and her hair is tangled. She buries her head so low that I can see the pink ribbon tied on the back of her hair, and I know she is desperately in need of a friend.

'Look at Amy,' I say to my friend Megan. 'She is miserable.'

'Un-huh,' Megan replies. 'So what?'

'Seriously, I think she needs help.'

Megan laughs. 'What are you? Mother Teresa?'

'Can we go sit with her?' It takes me a while to pluck up the courage to ask.

'Don't be silly.'

'I'm not kidding.' I stare at her.

Megan sits up, stares back, and lowers her voice. 'Where the heck did you get this idea from? She is messing with Christina!'

'So?' I whisper. 'Christina is a bully.'

'Everyone knows that Amy has taken her place in the summer camp,' she whispers back to me.

'Come on! It's an Art Camp, and Amy is more qualified. That's why they chose her.'

'Well, try to explain that to Christina,' Megan intimidates me. 'Good luck!'

'So are you coming with me or not?'

'Of course not,' Megan replies.

That's it. Without another word, I pick up my plate and walk away.

To be honest, I do feel nervous. 'Group Isolation' is Christina's usual punishment for those who piss her off, and my decision to break the rules will definitely offend her. Everybody says it would be a privilege to be her friend, but I believe she will never become my friend. Christina is smart, pretty, and taller than most girls of our age, but these things do not make her a good person.

There, Amy is living proof of her tyranny. She was left in the corner for almost two weeks. Two weeks without a single person to talk to must be painful. I try to imagine myself in her shoes, and it makes me tremble. 'I must help her,' it comes to my mind. 'Otherwise, if I were left like that someday, nobody would care for me.'

Amy's eyes pop when she sees me sit down in front of her, but after a moment of hesitation, she smiles at me with her tiny, white teeth.

I try to find a way to open the conversation. 'The bacon smells awful. Don't you think?'

'Um, yes.' She sounds timid.

Then we fall into an awkward silence. Amy and I have never talked much in the past, so we are not sure what can be a safe topic. Amy scratches the tips of her nails with unease, and after gathering her courage, she asks me, 'Would you like some ice cream?'

'Well, yes, I mean, why not?'

'I'm going for dessert.' She stands up and smiles. 'I'll get you some.'

'Thanks,' I say.

She responds with a bigger smile, and walks to the dessert table. Her steps are bouncy, sandals flapping against the ground with an amusing rhythm. Her bright-coloured school dress swings, leaving a delightful whirl in the air.

Then I see Christina, surrounded by girls who hold their ballerina postures, looking at me. Following Christina's eyes, the girls all start to stare at me. Their heads are raised so high that I feel they're looking at me with their nostrils. I turn back, pretending not to have seen anything.

Amy is back. She gives me a bowl filled with ice cream: a vanilla scoop, a chocolate scoop, and a mint chip scoop. 'I didn't know which flavour you'd prefer, so I got one of each.'

She blushes and smiles again. It makes me feel easy and comfortable.

And that day before she leaves, she says, 'Thank you for being here with me.'

'Mama, look! I'm a knight!' I waved my plastic sword in the air.

I was five then. The helmet was a folded paperboard box, painted with bronze pigment. The cloak was cut from my old bedroom curtain. The armor, of course, was made from a pair of window blinds. It wasn't easy to wear the costume tight and keep myself from tumbling around.

'All I need is a pony,' I announced, 'to save people and become a hero.'

'Look at her,' Mama said to her friends. 'Isn't she cute?'

During the class break next day, when I head to the bathroom, Christina follows me with her friends. Without any other choice, I ignore her, go straight to a stall, and lock the door.

Yet after I pee, I realize the problem: they blocked my door from outside.

I push, I knock, and I yell, 'Help!' I get no answer, only giggles.

'Let me out!' I punch the door. 'It's not funny! I have to go to class!'

Still no one answers, but I hear someone come in to the room, her little leather heels clicking on the floor, and she says, 'Hi Christina!' It's Megan's voice.

'Megan!' I cry out. 'Help me! get me out of here!'

'Um, what is happening?' Megan asks.

'None of your business.' It's Christina's voice.

'Help me open the door, Megan!' I shout.

Silence is her response.

'Megan!' I call out even louder.

'Sorry Megan,' Christina suddenly speaks. 'I didn't mean to yell at you.'

'It's fine,' Megan says. 'You didn't yell.'

'Megan.' My voice sounds faint.

I don't know what is happening behind the door, but I hear Megan say, 'Sorry, Stella.'

Then I hear the bathroom door creak. Together, their footsteps disappear.

Our class will start in two minutes, but I'm still trapped in this humiliating place. The smell of urine and menstrual blood lingers in the air, and the light bulb hanging above my head seems dim and rotten.

The whole bathroom is quiet, and I can hear water drip down from the faucet into the sink, echoing around the whole room. Then I hear another creaking sound. Someone comes in.

'Help!' I cry. 'I'm stuck in this stall.'

I hear her steps get close, and she stands on the other side of the door. 'Who are you? Why are you in there?' Her voice sounds familiar.

'I will tell you later,' I say. 'Can you help me with the door first?'

I cling to the door, trying not to miss any response, but I get nothing. 'Please,' I say, 'open the door. I promise I'll pay you back.'

The person doesn't reply. I can only hear the the rustle of her shoes, so I lower my body to the ground, and peek out under the door. I see bare feet with pink nail polish, wearing a pair of sandals with long, white laces. God bless me, it's Amy!

'Amy,' I call to her. 'Is that you?'

The anxious movement of her feet suddenly stops.

'I'm Stella!' I cry out excitedly.

'I'm not Amy,' the person says. But now I can tell, it's clearly Amy's voice.

I watch the movement of her feet. She takes a step forward, but stops halfway. Then she seems to regret her decision, so she steps back, and says, 'I'm sorry.'

'Amy,' I say, 'help me.'

Suddenly the bell rings, and I see the feet turn back and run away. She is farther and farther from me, and my vision expands from her feet to her shank, the pleats of her dress, the edge of her hair, and the back of her head.

Now, I finally see her for who she is.

'Mama,' I said. 'The bird is going to die.'

A tiny sparrow. I found her in the yard. Her feathers are falling off her wings. She might have bumped into an electric web. She wouldn't live long.

I poured out everything from my pencil box, and stuffed it with a thin layer of grass. By the side, I put a bottle cap of water and some millet. Did she like her new room or not? I couldn't tell. She barely ate or drank anything. The next morning, she was lying stiff in the box.

I dug a hole in our backyard and buried her. I sat by her side and sang her a lullaby. I keep a feather of hers in my drawer, and stroke it when I think of her.

'Look at her,' that's what Mama said to her friends. 'Isn't she cute?'

MAKING FRIENDS
Josh Simpson

He arrived in pieces and the head came first. I reached into the box and felt coarse, curly hair, pulled on it to lift it out, and saw it was a rusty colour that complimented the soft skin.

I'd just warmed up some pasta and I put the head in front of my plate. The first bite of pasta was cold and his eyes stared at me. I reached up to pull down the eyelids. One stayed down while the other slowly peeled back up, so that half his face seemed to slowly wake before freezing into a wink, as though he'd just told a joke and was looking at me in good humour. That simply wouldn't do, the cold pasta or the frozen face, so I threw away one and put the other back in his box.

The rest of him did not immediately arrive after the head, which gave me time to finish preparing his room. I'd chosen a soft yellow, a nice, neutral colour he might like. Just in case he didn't like it, I'd also bought cans of blue and white, stacked in the closet, and would let him choose. Maybe I should've let him choose before painting at all, but I couldn't bear the thought of him seeing the room for the first time as something bare, naked, cold. So, in addition to the paint, I added a bed and large bookcase, though I hadn't yet bought any books for it.

I pulled the head from the box and set it on one of the empty shelves, his face still frozen in that wink, one eye staring at the yellow of the wall across from it. His rusty hair and pale skin clashed with the yellow, and I realized I would have to paint the room blue even if he liked the yellow. I left him on that shelf and closed the door, opening it only in the mornings before I left and in the evenings when I arrived home.

Six days later, the doorbell rang while I was showering and I knew his fingers had come. Water dripped onto hardwood as I collected the package from the door, pushed my thumb into the middle of the box and tore it open. Foam packing spilled out and I plucked from it each finger, one by one. There were six total: two thumbs, two forefingers, two index fingers. You probably already knew that fingers were expensive, so I'd limited myself to just three per hand. I could always order more. Or maybe someone would get them for my birthday in seven months. By then I could've made some friends, couldn't I? We'd laugh and have good times and they'd all ask what I wanted for my thirty-fifth and I'd tell them all about the fingers and we'd laugh some more and maybe then I wouldn't need him.

The torso and arms came next. The legs arrived last since they had been on backorder. I pushed my couch and coffee table to the wall and spread each body part around the living room. His head was still in the box in his room, had leaked through the bottom of the cardboard so I put him in upside down until I was ready. In that moment, though, I just stared at all the parts strewn about. The two legs draped over either side of the couch. The arms made a U shape on the carpet and the two hands held each other. It was rather touching and I wondered if he would be someone I could love. He would be there every day when I came home. Would he eat cold pasta? Would he eat at all?

I didn't look forward to reading the instructions so I left him like that for a few more days, allowing my anticipation to build before finally putting him together. Once everything seemed to be in its place, I stood him up and said hello.

'Bonjour,' he said, and the other eye popped open. At first, his eyes were a soft grey so pale they almost blended into the white of the scleras. Then the irises slowly transitioned, clockwise, from grey to amber-green. When the transformation was complete, he suddenly seemed alive, popping with intelligence. I forgot he'd even spoken, I was so startled by the change.

'Bonjour,' he said again.

I blinked. 'Bonjour?'

'Bonjour.'

'You speak English, don't you?' I looked around for the instructions, thinking perhaps I'd missed a switch somewhere.

'Ça va?' he asked, taking a step forward. I noticed his left leg was a bit loose and wondered what would happen if I pushed him over.

'Yeah, sure,' I said, glancing over the instructions and seeing nothing about language. I called the manufacturer and explained that I'd ordered English.

'Sorry, sir, we cannot guarantee language.'

'That's absurd.'

'Sorry, sir, but our terms and conditions explain that language preferences are met only when possible and cannot be guaranteed. You may wish to review the terms and conditions, sir.'

I vaguely recalled checking some box when I placed the order and my face flushed with heat. I'd heard about things like this happening and I thought about how much he'd cost. 'No one reads that shit, you know. Why do you even offer a fucking preference if you're just going to send whatever you want?'

'Sorry, sir, but please do not use that language with me.'

'What, you prefer it in French?' I asked before ending the call.

I looked over at him and he stared at his loose leg, tapped it with one hand, then raised both hands and stared at them. 'Mes doigts?'

After that, we spent most of our time together in silence:

staring at each other over dinner (he ate four small, turquoise pellets that powered him for seven and a half hours); watching television; him watching me get ready for bed before I locked him in his room. Every once in awhile, I'd catch him staring at his hands.

I started learning French at night, while he was locked away, and on my drive to work. Eventually, I learned enough to understand when he was asking for the rest of his fingers. I pretended I still didn't speak his language.

PORTAL TO THE SOUL

James Machell

Doreen576 awoke in the darkness of her coffin, 26th century slang for sleeping pods, and a metal stranger was dreaming beside her. His eyes were open, and looked like pebbles, because Android's lost control of their eyelids after shutting down. But she could see the dull globes with her night vision. The lid slid to one side, when it sensed consciousness, flooding them with light and activating a sensor that made him start blinking. Androids were kept in the kitchen because the household wasn't as big as some of the others, but it was convenient for her to make coffee for herself or the family's breakfast. After pouring two cups there had still been no further reaction from him other than fluttering eye-lashes, so she spoke, her voice electric and beautiful.

'I love you.'

'I love you too,' he answered, stirring. 'But my Master will want me soon.'

'Can't you stay for breakfast?'

'I eat with him and his family. He won't be happy if my appetite is gone.' He got up and unashamed by nudity, drained the steaming mug before slipping into white overalls. They were both new models and designed to be more attractive than humans could ever hope to be.

'What is your name?' she asked.

'Why do you ask?'

'So I know you if I see you again.' Owing to large scale manufacturing, products of each brand shared looks and personality, so they were hard to distinguish.

'It's Adam92.' He went through the automatic door and escaped her stony gaze.

His Master waited by the front door for him to enter.

'Where have you been?'

'With an FR[1] called Doreen.'

'You're late!' Adam92 displayed the clock in his arm and watched the Master slink away, having realised his mistake. A steel brain made it easy to interpret behaviour because there were no emotions clouding it. The Master was jealous of artificial promiscuity and sometimes wished that he'd been made in a factory.

The chef-bot, Robert627, presented a plate of runny eggs, blackened by pepper. The Mistress ate them, with toast, in a bad mood as usual. Every Friday she cried because she thought she had fat and was yet to realise how her moods followed a routine.

'These are awful,' she told Robert627 who always made them perfectly. The Mistress had killed the last chef with a broom, 11 Friday's ago, and he was afraid.

'I'm sorry,' he said and took the plate away.

Adam92 ate his in silence and ignored her eldest son who kicked him from under the table. His knee would have jerked if

---

1   Female Robot

it had been human.

'You look beautiful ma'am,' Robert627 said.

'Be quiet.'

The Master entered and put his hand on the back of her neck as if training a dog. 'We have a party tonight so be sure to dress up.'

'I'm too fat to go outside.'

'You're beautiful.' The Mistress was one of those rare people who looked fantastic with makeup but terrible without, broad nose and strong jaw. Most of the fuss she made was either to receive compliments or make people suffer.

'My friends are expecting you.'

'Tell them to shove it.' She stormed into the luxury bedroom, but the Master followed. After ten minutes of arguing she would explain how her mind had transformed him into a monster and she was lashing out at that. They would then make love and resume their lives as usual.

Adam92 gave Robert627 a knowing wink and they rejoiced about how they were better than people in at least one respect.

The laws of robotics made them subservient to biological flesh and it was a common fear that Androids could learn to disobey. Psychiatric wards were full of people who believed their tools only pretended to be subservient.

Adam92 thought about this when picking apples and was surprised to see Doreen576 at the other end of the orchard. The leaves were greenest in summer and her hair flowed like water in the wind.

'What do you want?' asked Adam92.

'I came to make an agreement.' She explained that it made sense to have relations again because it saved them a trip to the club, where Androids went without owners to recharge their batteries. Adam92 explained that the house would be free tonight and she should knock after the car had left. Doreen576 smiled and exposed a set of immaculate teeth.

He watched her disappear into the distance and focussed on her long silhouette against the blueberry sky.

'Are you real?' asked the Son as his parents readied for a party. Adam92 taught philosophy by encouraging him to ask questions but they quickly turned into insults.

'In the biological sense — Yes. But I'm not considered real by the IOR[2] for want of a soul. Even though I can think.'

'Is an apple real?'

'Probably less than me but arguably the same.' The Son was one of those children who thought they were handsome and clever because he had always been told so by his mother and nannies. He looked at Androids, and the other children at school, as inferior beings.

The Mistress came down, hot from a bath with a towel around her.

'Your stupid father is on the phone.' It was strange to Adam92 that the owners went to bed in each other's arms. He recalled the Master boasting about being woken with a kiss, even though Androids slept side by side and were never jealous nor admiring. 'Ask him to come down!' she told Adam92.

He obeyed and ultra-sensitive hearing led him to the Master in the second bedroom at the back of the house. He listened by the door before knocking and heard that the Master had a girlfriend, who he loved, and would see later that week:

'Goodnight my precious girl. You mustn't think about my wife. Suffering around her only makes me appreciate you more,' he whispered. 'And it kills me spending a moment apart from you when I know that we'll die someday and spend an eternity with our horrid spouses.'

The wood had barely been tapped when the Master was in

2   Institute of Robotics

Adam92's face, demanding that he stop skulking around.

'Your wife wants you to come downstairs.'

'My wife wants you dismantled! And if it was up to her you would never be allowed to leave the house.'

The IOR tried to incorporate human aspects into their products, including the need for recess and intimacy, so a refusal to allow this would be considered robot cruelty. There was no law against killing them though.

By the time his wife was dressed, they were both in better moods and held hands on the way out. The Son watched from the window as the car slipped from view.

'Are Mummy and Daddy friends?'

'They're married,' Adam92 replied.

He lulled the Son to sleep with stories of adventures in space that always culminated in the hero kissing an alien princess whom he never saw again.

Doreen576 arrived a short while later and rang the doorbell.

Owing to the considerable beauty of Androids, many buyers kept them in their original costume. She was dressed in white, as was Adam92. The radio had been left on and a slow recording was playing. It was carried to the coffin-room, by Adam92, because music was known to improve conversation. Because there were was only one other Android in his Master's employ, and Robert627 had his own room, he considered this his personal space, even though there was no art on the walls.

'Do you like art?' asked Adam92, observing the blankness of his room with a fresh perspective.

'No.'

'Why?'

'Because there's too much in a book or a painting. I like the taste of food and the smell of flowers.'

They joined lips and their minds shut down for fifteen minutes.

This was a profound rest and more fulfilling than an eternity of being switched off.

They lay like toys in a box until his owners returned. The car came noisily into the driveway and there was drunken laughter outside.

'You're like something from a movie,' the Mistress said as she stumbled through the front door.

'And you're so so nice.' The Master caressed her waist and went to the bedroom which became an area for cuddles and silly nothings. 'I hope I've made your life better,' he continued. 'I couldn't love you as much if that wasn't the case.'

A rocking sound permeated the old house and was then replaced by gentle snoring.

'People,' explained Doreen576, 'are all narcissists and crave adoration above everything else. Only they're also ambitious and territorial so they never get what they want and this makes them angry. I'm glad I'm a machine even though I won't go to Heaven.'

Adam92 looked into her green orbs and saw a flicker behind the mechanism.

SURPRISE

Rachana Bhattacharjee

Jeff is standing at a blind-spot between two street-lights. The street is deserted. The sun set an hour ago, fireflies and crickets are out and about on the streets. It's quiet all around except for faint music and a murmur of merry conversation wafting out from the large window of the house he's looking straight at. Cheerful people wearing pearls and tuxedos are dancing and chatting. His daughter, Sarah, is with a girl her age. They're laughing together. The girl opens her purse and pulls out a small paper package. She unwraps it, revealing a purple dog collar. She runs her fingers over a brown bone-shaped bow on it, explaining something. Sarah looks around. Jeff breathes a chuckle and stamps out his cigarette.

'I don't know, Poppins must've gone out to the garden to dig up his bone from under the lilies,' Jeff says, softly, in a high-pitched, sing-song way, following Sarah's lips. He whispers another chuckle and walks around to the back of the dumpster he was leaning on. He runs his hands on the large gift-wrapped box that is kept concealed there. It's half as tall as him. He is six feet and hefty, clean shaven now, even his head; wearing a set of clothes he's stolen from somebody's closet a few blocks away. There is a slight slouch to his posture and his eyes are so tired they've taken shelter in dark caves in his now gaunt face. He has been preparing for this day for a while, re-playing it in his head. He blows into his palms and takes a whiff of his breath: Whisky and smoke. His pockets are empty. Damn it; he's left the box of peppermints on his rug. He throws his head back in exasperation, but instead of stars he is faced with a scanty swarm of flies zooming about just above his nose. He blinks a few times and twitches his nose vigorously to ward them off. It's eerie how close they are, how close they were to his head; droning, darting around, as though they're measuring his demeanour and analyzing the data to uncover his thoughts. He finds the fingers of his right hand rubbing his chin. It feels a little ticklish; he's used to combing a tangle of rough hair, not caressing smooth skin. He continues to stare at the flies. The hypnotic effect of watching them gives him solace. He fixates on the one zigzagging closest to his face; teases it by following it with his nose. He is about to make an attempt to catch it in his mouth when a shooting itch in his other arm, on the forearm, causes him to flinch. Must've been a mosquito. He sighs, picks up the parcel and trudges towards the door. He stops by the bed of lilies on the way, plucks one and closes his eyes while drawing in and absorbing its scent. It's intoxicating. But it's not enough. He plucks another and then another; loses himself in their fragrance, too, for a few minutes.

He pushes them into the ribbon on the parcel, smiles, and begins walking again. The sound of claps and cheers reach his ears.

'No need to be alarmed,' he announces on entering. He kicks the door shut, and puts the parcel down. The joviality and the music has considerably calmed his nerves.

Every back in the room twists, then turns, then freezes; either stern or gaping. He's expected this; it's a replay of what happened repeatedly for a year every time he walked down this street, or into the local supermarket, until a few weeks ago, when he decided to permanently move into a den on the edge of the town.

'Beth?' he calls.

There's no response.

'Happy birthday,' he sings.

Some people on the fringes of the room whisper to each other.

'I've brought you a gift,' he declares.

No one moves.

'As soon as Beth accepts my gift, I'll be on my way. I come in peace, I promise,' he explains to the guests.

A few seconds pass. A woman in her fifties, his ex-wife, inches forward, revealing herself from behind the kitchen wall. He can see her quivering in fear. She better be. She seems to have forgotten he exists, forgotten who he is; buying happiness at the cost of his.

'Hello Beth,' he says, gently, in his most reassuring voice.

'Wh — why are you here?'

He can see her swallow a large helping of saliva. 'I've brought you a gift. Won't you open it?' He smiles. 'Happy birthday, Beth.' He takes a step towards her. She is visibly trembling now, almost on the verge of tears.

'Dad!'

He stops short; turns sharply to the voice. Sarah has stepped out from behind the kitchen wall, too, and is walking towards him. She is rigid, her fists are clenched, her jaw is taught. But Jeff's eyes are drawn to the half-cut cake beyond her shoulder. His stomach rumbles.

'My darling,' he smiles, forcing himself to focus on her. She is such a beautiful girl.

She surprises him by wrapping her arms around him. 'It's good to see you, Daddy. What have you got here for mum that's so big?'

Sarah shrugs away her mother who is trying to pull her back. Beth is terrified of him. Good. Not Sarah: She is his little girl. She knows he wouldn't hurt her. He is lucky to have such a smart and sweet little girl. The hug reassures him: Perhaps he hasn't lost her after all, despite Beth's efforts.

'Can *I* open it?' Sarah asks.

He lets out a heavy breath. There is a constriction in his throat. He doesn't want to have to do this to Sarah. 'Why don't you let your mum do it?'

Beth is standing supported by another woman now. He knows her. She's from the neighbourhood. The one who'd held Beth on another night: the night he'd been arrested for drunken abuse of his spouse. She was there to send him on his way even on the day he'd come back to apologise, after his release. '*Beth* was going through a trauma,' she'd said to him. Yeah, right!

'Hey, leave them alone,' a man yells from Jeff's left.

Jeff turns to him and glares, cracking his knuckles.

'I'll open it,' Sarah says quickly. 'Mum's not feeling quite well.'

She tears off the first layer of wrapping, uncovering a cardboard carton that opens on the side. She looks up at him as though impressed by what he's achieved. She ought to be. He's worked hard to put it together. There is a second carton inside (Beth's sobs and the other lady's 'shh's are becoming quite bothersome). And inside that, a third (Jeff has begun to scratch at the skin above his left thumbnail). Then a fourth (What a scene! Can't a man bring a birthday gift in peace?). Sarah brings out the last box; approximately the size of a microwave.

'A bone on the ribbon,' she exclaims and places the box on the floor, a smile flickering on her lips. But Jeff is watching Beth keenly; he doesn't catch her words.

Sarah rips off the wrapper. His thumb is bleeding; it stings. If only she'd hurry up. But, then, perhaps he shouldn't have used so many boxes. He could've kept one to spread on the floor below his rug in his den. It would've helped with the cold. Beth has turned a deathly pale. He hopes she won't faint before the prize is revealed. Sarah slowly lifts the piece of black blanket that he's covered the object with, a piece of the only thing he has been able to call home for the past year: His rug.

Gasps echo through the room. Sarah screams and backs away.

Beth faints.

The gift is a small cage containing a Labrador puppy in a pool of sticky, half-dried blood. It is cold and still; its eyes mere glossy black buttons, its claws spread out in tension, a large gash on its throat. Its fur is still silky and golden.

'When she comes to, you tell her, Sarah, you tell your mum,' Jeff says slowly, pointing to Poppins' corpse, 'that this is for her. For being a dear and sending me to hell. Now, she can have all the parties she wants. Just know that I'm still out here. You tell her, Sarah. You tell her. And you know I love you. This is not your fault. You'll be alright. You'll be alright.'

He nods and walks out onto the street. He breaks into a laugh, then a run. He doesn't stop until he's turned the corner. That was a good show. But there is one last errand to run; he needs to leave an apology note at the house from which he's stolen the clothes. He wonders why that slipped his mind before.

THE LEGEND OF SIR WILLIAM
JETHRO MARSHAL
Mark Flanagan

Verily, the yarn of mine fateful duel can be said to have begun the eve prior, in the vaunted halls of goodly Master Fowler, the chemistry teacher. My compatriots and I were gathered anon to engage in a battle of wits, using the time-honored tradition of the logical debate as is customary on Thursdays following school. As we waited for M. Fowler to arrive, a gasp arose from a small gathering around Brother Quentin. Fearing danger, I steeled myself and made my way into the throng. With a nod at his iPhone, thus Quentin spake:

'Dude, look at the shit that Fletch just posted about Abby.'

Upon the glittering screen formed the image of the most foul 'Rate Me MGHS' page, first wrought into existence by mine mortal enemy, the bastard Fletcher Kay. This was a cruel device used by the students of Maple Grove High School to establish an oppressive hierarchy of rankings, from a single star to ten stars. Below the WordArt banner was the profile of Abigail Garcia-

Roth, her image a balm to my weary soul. Her long, midnight locks curled in tight ringlets and shone with a luminousness that would put the stars in heaven to shame. Her nose and brow seemed carved from moonstone, aquiline and proud, and above all, *regal*. Such beauty! Long had she held my heart captive, and long had I held my tongue. Below this radiant portrait, mine eye saw the unthinkable, a score of one star.

Lies! Trickery! Deceit! Such a beautiful creature could not possibly receive a score so low! I myself was the recipient of many one and two star ratings, but the lion did not concern himself with the opinions of sheep. That is of course, provided the sheep did not seek to slander the reputation of the saintly Abigail. Below the altered score sat Fletcher's review, its devilish scribblings an assault on my very senses. T'was writ thusly:

'Don't let the good girl routine fool you, Abby is a total slut. She thinks she can get away with w/e she wants bcuz her parents are rich. Think again bitch. I'll be releasing nudes of this beat-ass girl @ 9pm tomorrow if anyone's interested. HMU on Twitter @deeznuts6969.'

'How is this possible?' I queried.

Quentin didst speak, 'Fletcher runs the site man; he can change anything however he wants.'

Oh, how I railed against the injustice! If only dearest Abigail could but see the depths of my affection, surely she wouldst succumb to mine gentlemanly charm. I didst hammer my hands upon the blood-red lockers with my gaze to the heavens, seeking the answers writ there, but the cold fluorescent lights offered no warmth, nor suggestions. Overcome by a sickness of the soul and fraught with worry for mine Guinevere, I didst abandon the scholars of the debate team, returning to my homestead upon my trusty steed, the Mongoose XP-12.

After a goodly feast of macaroni and cheese and liquid repast of Mountain Dew, I retired to my study in my mother's basement. Surely within these stacks of comics, dusty fantasy tomes and monster manuals was the secret to mine success. I reread for the thousandth time the brave exploits of Lancelot in White's *The Once and Future King*. Oh how beloved Lancelot was of me, the ugly knight who wins the heart of his queen through his brave exploits and kind heart. Filled with self-loathing was he, as I could be when perhaps reading yet another poorly review on the dreaded Rate Me MGHS page. That foul page. A growl didst rise in mine throat as my thoughts turned to the rival of my brief life:

Fletcher Kay.

That treacherous weasel thought he could besmirch the honor of my queen-to-be? T'was in *The History of French Chivalry* that I found my solution. The author didst speak of the last legal duel in France between Jean de Carrouges and Jacques Le Gris over charges of matrimonial rape.

Were not the slanderous words of Fletcher Kay tantamount to rape? Not a rape of the body but of the spirit, of the reputation? I didst resolve then and there that I, William Jethro Marshal, would duel Fletcher Kay for the honor of darling Abigail. I would visit upon him the wrath of a thousand suns, and by my hand he would know defeat. He wouldst kneel before me and beg for his pathetic life, and I wouldst whisper 'no.' That night I slept soundly, mind alight with imaginings of the passionate kiss Abigail would bestow upon me, my very first, after I smote Fletcher's ruin upon the ninth grade hall.

I awoke sore after the manly amount of pushups I didst do. Then I didst shower and anoint myself with holy oils and shaved off the patchy beard I had been favoring. I didst don my armor, the black Duster of Impenetrability and the Trilby of Invulnerability. A hearty feast of Eggos didst comprise my breakfast, and with a gladsome wink to dearest mother, I mounted mine steed and made fast towards the fortress where my beloved and my destiny awaited me.

Up and down the hallways I didst stalk, searching for mine enemy and making preparations for this rash act. Lo, I didst find him near his locker, surrounded by his army of cronies. Terrible to behold was he, lithe of body, skin scaled with fake tan, black cowlick weighed down upon with much unguent and hair product, armored in a Nike 'Just Do It' shirt and Nantucket red pantaloons. As the twin dimples appeared on his sinister countenance, I felt a most terrible anger arise in my breast. Of what use was my life, if not to use my superior heroism to mete out justice and uphold righteousness? What form of man would allow the defenseless Abigails of the world to wander unprotected, forever victim to the Fletcher's of the world? I was pulled from my furious reverie by a taunt from my mortal enemy:

'Hey, Dildo Faggins, quit staring at me, shit's freaky.'

Ah Fletcher, a finer example of what the laymen might call a 'douche bag' has never walked upon this green earth. Quoth I:

'Fletcher Kay, I challenge you to trial by combat for the slander of Abigail Garcia-Roth and attempted rape of her character. You may choose no champion to fight in your stead. Our fight will be to the death. Do you accept these terms?'

Laughter came bleating out of the mouths of those sheep nearest mine foe. Quoth he:

'Jesus Christ Jethblow, are you asking me to kick your scrawny ass in front of the entire school? Because that's what this sounds like.'

I dropped into the Heart of Stone, feeling my emotions drain away, leaving behind naught but cold anger and purpose. Towards the wretch I didst walk when, like the sun breaking through the clouds, the shining face of Abigail didst appear, her eyes still red from a night of crying. Merely seeing her gaze upon me threatened to break my considerable concentration and control, but alas, my course was set. Before Fletcher could level another insult at me, I didst grab him by his lame attire and shoved him hard against the locker-walled arena. His visage took on an appearance most hilarious, before settling into a scowl.

'Alright you fucking freak you asked for this.'

A great cheer arose from the crowd as we two deadly combatants circled each other. We did this for some time, neither daring to make the first move. I chanced a swing at his head. One, two, one, two and through and through, the vorpal strike went slipper-slap! Seizing this opportunity, he returned a slap to him own face and then didst tackle me to the ground. Oh what mighty blows were exchanged whenst rolling upon the floor!

THE LEGEND OF SIR WILLIAM JETHRO MARSHAL

Knees met crotches, hands met faces, teeth met shoulders. From the lowest dungeon to the highest peak I fought him, until I felt myself ascending by the scruff of mine tabard.

Who should the hand belong to but goodly Master Fowler, though his eyes bespoke a terrible rage.

'What the hell is this?'

Quoth I, 'Tis a trial by combat for the honor of Abigail. He didst seek to slander her good name…'

'Jesus, Fletcher, is this that website again? I swear this is it mister, you've been…'

The noble teacher's words and the protestation of Fletcher didst fall away before my ears, as my eyes drifted towards splendid Abigail in the crowd. Freeing myself from Fowler's clutches, I ran to her and kneeled.

'M'lady, if you would deign to give your lowly servant but a single kiss for his travails, I would be most glad.'

More bleating from the sheep. Quoth she 'Jeez, William, it's not like we've ever really talked to each other, and I appreciate the gesture, but I don't really feel comfortable kissing you.' She didst shrug. 'Sorry.'

Unbelievable. What a bitch.

METRO

Megan Jones

The dress is perfect. I mean, okay, the colour isn't what I would normally go for – the red is a bit more salacious than my usual taste, and I feel like there's a siren going off somewhere vaguely in the background as I walk around the room, and alright, it is a little tight, under the arms and across the back, and yes, now I think about it I would have expected €120 to buy something in a material that feels a little less scratchy, but who cares, because I look great. He's going to love it. I know he'll appreciate the effort I went to and all the little things I put into this night to make sure it's special, because I know he's as nervous as I am that this is our last night together. He's going to love it.

I decide to wear my hair down but it's flapping all heavy and thick around my neck and making me so hot I feel like I might sweat right out of this dress. The longer I spend in here the sweatier I get so fuck it, that'll do, I look great, I really do.

I walk into our living room slowly, deliberately clattering the lock on the bathroom door and clicking my heels on the wooden floor so he'll turn around and get the full effect of *the dress* and me in it but he's fiddling with his keys, *At last, are you ready?* and yes fair enough I've been in there for hours, although it's weird that in all the time I've been in there he didn't change his shirt or brush his teeth. He doesn't mention anything about the dress but in fairness I've just put my coat on now and you can't really see it. I'm sure he'll say something when we get to the restaurant.

This place used to be my favourite when I lived here last year I say when we're on the Metro, because I want to remind him that I've lived in Paris before but I think he actually just rolled his eyes, although in fact it could be that he was just reading that advert over there, although actually it's about impotence so maybe not. It's not something he has ever had a problem with in my experience; I mean some weekends I think *Is this really what we came to Paris for, I like sex but six times in one day is probably enough don't you think and wouldn't you like to go see the Jardin du Luxembourg?* But what do I know, I've never had a boyfriend before and at least now I can have realistic expectations for next time because this time is already winding down. It wasn't an entirely mutual decision because I don't think Germany is really that far away and you can get those £9.99 flights from Ryanair. But he was insistent that it wouldn't work and that we'd just hold each other back although I have to say that if anyone was being held back it would be me because I've just got this great new job that pays an obscene amount of money and actually I'm moving into a huge white flat in the Seizième, and he's moving into a room that some middle aged lady rents out in Leipzig to do an unpaid internship, so if I don't have a problem with it then why should he. But I don't want to rehash old arguments because this is our last night so I shouldn't waste time arguing about decisions that have already been made.

I think I'll have the Prawn Cocktail I say. I took my coat off nearly twenty minutes ago now but he hasn't said anything about the dress, maybe it does look really cheap, I never know with these things, my thighs are really uncomfortably sweaty under the table and if I move one of them they actually make this embarrassing little squeaking noise so maybe the dress was a mistake after all because I feel like I'm wearing a huge scarlet bandage and if people are looking at all it's probably not in a nice way, and he isn't looking anyway. He hasn't said a word since we left the apartment, and although I understand he must be finding this impending separation really hard he could maybe channel it differently, like me – I'm trying to be positive and making a big effort with my appearance rather than being all silent and moody. I decide to be quiet for a while but it doesn't last very long because I actually don't really like being quiet, and maybe I don't know very much about relationships but I don't think you're supposed to go out for a meal and sit in silence when you've only been together for six months, that seems like the sort of thing that should happen after six years or not even then. So I talk to the waiter instead, and despite opinions to the contrary I know my French has got a lot better since we moved here because I always make the effort to talk to people because that's how you learn.

The prawn cocktail is very good and I almost say that out loud but then I don't because it might fall under the umbrella of *pointless interjections*, which according to some people I make a lot of, so instead I look around the room at the other couples in the restaurant and count how many of them are a) sitting in silence or b) under the age of twenty five and there are about ten of each but in a Venn diagram there wouldn't be much crossover between the two groups and I start thinking that maybe it would be better if we were arguing because then it would mean that one of us hadn't just been completely beaten into submission by the other.

When we've finished eating we get the bill and I offer to pay because I'm the one getting this obscene salary although I won't actually start getting it until next month and I also wasn't the one who ordered the chateaubriand for two and then ate it all myself but I don't mind. *I thought maybe we could go up the Eiffel Tower, we've lived here for three months and we've never done it* I say and he gives me this look like he isn't even going to justify my question with an answer but then realises he has to and says *I don't feel good, I think I ate too much* to which I respond *But it's our last night!* To which he says *That doesn't mean I feel good* so I walk him to the Metro and call *See you at home!* to the back of his head and walk over to the Tower by myself. I go up and take some pictures but it's the sort of thing that looks better from the ground than from the top and

I end up deleting the pictures anyway and then I just feel like a stupid tourist in a very badly-fitting red dress who has been left to do this Parisian rite of passage by herself.

I go down into the Metro, but it's only been half an hour since he left and I don't want to go home right away because I want it to seem like I've had a nice evening by myself. So I let a few trains go past and I look at the people in them and I wonder how many of them are going home to someone and how many are going home alone, and how many of them wish they were going home alone when in fact they're going home to someone, and the other way around, and how you probably never appreciate one or the other when it's happening to you.

One train is sitting at the station for ages and I see that there's a very attractive man sitting inside it, opposite me where I sit on the platform. At first I think he's looking at me because he can see up my skirt but then I realise he's looking at my face and my hair and the dress and he seems to be liking what he's seeing. He nods and then I smile and nod back but then look away quickly because I have a boyfriend, but then look back again because very soon I won't have one. The train is still at the platform and he seems like he's deciding whether to get off or not when suddenly the doors close and the train slides away. He waves at me regretfully and I wave back enthusiastically. The tunnel is dark again and I'm thinking you know actually £9.99 really is quite a lot of money when you think about it, because just think how many Metro tickets you can buy with that.

HOMECOMING

Thea Marie Rishovd

She drives past the intersection every day, never turning left. White headlights and blue metal. Staying close but never within reach. When she walked out the door Tom crumbled to a useless, deflated heap of heartache and misery. I thought surely she'd come back, otherwise the door handle would have turned round and round, and round.

I am hidden by a bundle of oak trees, just off the main road. Two stories of white walls and blue windows, I rise out of the shrubbery, blocking the view of the sea behind. If you approach from the south the wall is painted red up to about halfway up the first floor. Another tick on the list of what Tom couldn't do right. Now the paint is peeling away in flakes. Red shavings falling like drops of blood into the grass below. It's not a good look, I know.

Eventually Tom and I came to an understanding. I kept the water running, and Tom stopped trying to leave. It cost him a couple of fingers, and stained my windowsill a deep red, but we got there in the end. Electricity, like a constant itch, breathes life into the TV, the landline and the record player she left behind. As a bonus it gives me ample opportunity to play with the lights.

A deliveryman comes by every Monday with the necessities for the week. This took some trial and error, but eventually we managed a phone call without 'Please, you have to help me —', and agreed on a shopping list. It became a well-rehearsed routine. I slowly open a window, keeping an eye on Tom as he stands with his back against the wall on the other side of the room, and wait while the deliveryman puts the box through the window onto the kitchen counter. When he's done I let the window drop, making sure to have the lock turn at least once.

I mean, what's the use of Tom if he won't call her? When she first left I tried to just scare him. Had doors creak open at all hours of the night, turned his football games to static, locked him in the basement once. Thought he might call her for help. Beg her to come back. But he didn't. He tried to call the police once, but unfortunately there was a problem with the connection. I swear I just needed a way to convince her to walk back through my door. You can spot the flaw, I'm sure. If I opened the door to let her in, Tom could slip out and scare her away, and then I would lose them both. I would be all alone.

It took a lot of planning. I almost got ahead of myself, abandoning caution and patience in favour of a quick solution. If only I could get him to stick his head out the window, it would be over in a jiffy, but it occurred to me at the last minute that barring the lucky appearance of a hungry fox or wolf, or the quick work of the neighbouring crows, a severed head would be quite the warning sign for potential visitors. So I had to rethink. Now, if I may say so myself, it was an excellent plan. Noiselessly open one of the loft windows. Preferably the one on the south side, to encourage the birds. Wait for one of the bloody birds to fly in. Let it fumble in the wind for a bit, trying to get out, making the rats run for cover. Bang the window shut, careful not to shatter the glass. Accompany the screeches of the frightened bird with the occasional blast of the opening notes of 'O Fortuna' from

Orff's Carmina Burana, her favourite, left on the turntable in her hurry to leave. Watch as he jumps, hesitates, then opens the hatch, pulls down the ladder and climbs up. To be honest, I'm not too bothered about the state of the loft. But the ladder. The ladder I have kept in perfect condition. Keeping a careful eye on the rats. No gnawing here. The rest of the floor, however: I won't guarantee your safety if you walk on it. The loft has been left mostly empty since Tom threw out what remained of his mother's belongings. Luckily, after carrying a particularly heavy box of books outside, more fuel for the fire burning at the water's edge, he never bothered to look up here again. In the middle of the dusty room, full of rat droppings and bird feathers, there is an old lamp, yellow bulb surrounded by purple screen ringed by delicate bobbin lace. The bulb and the screen are held up by the head and the arms of a troll made of wood, a sly grin on its face. The lamp is made further remarkable by a long white wire. So long that it becomes an eyesore in any room. But, as they say, everything has its uses. A creek here, an unexpected loose floorboard there, a crow screech here, a white noose there.

I admit, there was the small problem of his feet sticking out of the roof of the room below. Like a chandelier. Fortunately, the picturesque view of the water, and the snowpeaked mountain in the distance, designated this the guest room, reserved for distinguished distant family members, who rarely graced us with their presence. Now it stands as a forgotten monument to my former glory. Potential guests will now find the door stuck, as if it has grown a size too big.

It's a small trick, really. Imitating his voice on the phone. You see, when he talked into the mouthpiece I would feel the vibrations, the transmission of sound waves tickling me, and I would savour my favourite words, saving them for later, replaying them. A poor substitute for the music she enjoyed, but at least Tom was finally being useful.

'Please…come…home.' An intake of breath. Was that a step too far? The home just slipped out.

'One last time…say goodbye.' Would he say that? No. He

would rather sit in his armchair and rot. The only good thing he ever did was bring her here. I finally let the rats loose on the tasty mahogany of the ladder, and they completely ignore it in favour of Tom's head. His eyes, in particular, a delicacy, apparently.

I haven't heard her voice in such a long time. It's icier than I remember. Less kind.

'There's nothing left to say. Please leave me alone.'

Serves me right for praying she would grow a backbone and cut him loose, I guess. There's no trace of emotion in her voice. Does her face betray her? Just a small act of imagination. I see her biting her lip, her pulse jumping. Her fingers curled around the receiver, nails scratching the plastic. Does this kind of thing happen in the books she reads? Does the music she listens to inspire her to imagine something like me? That's it.

'You left a couple of your music records here. Thought you… like them back.'

For a long time there is only her breath. Then, there's a clipped 'Fine, I'll come by after work' before she hangs up. In my joy, I forget myself and my windows get away from me. Doors swing on their hinges. The loft window sends a flock of birds into the sky, screeching. The wind hooks its fingers around the windowsills and pulls. My walls creek. Stretch. My foundations are firm, I have deep roots. A little spring cleaning is good for the soul, Tom's mother used to say, though she never cleaned anything in her life. She just opened every window and every door, and let the wind do the rest. It always took my breath away.

Now I wait patiently. I listen through Carmina Burana three times, as loudly as possible, letting the music merge with the wind. I sense the wheels of her car against the gravel of the drive before I notice the headlights glaring. Quickly there is silence. I hear the faint notes of music drifting out of the open car window. I can't hear the words of the song but I remember the tune. She used to fall asleep to this song on the days he was away for work. The music comes slowly closer. A tremor goes through me, and I hold on tight to door handles, hinges and locks.

Don't scare her away now.

I'D BE MUCH BETTER THERE

Cassidy Colwell

How many games of solitaire had I played today? Enough that the light from the window had moved from across the room, over my bed, and I could watch the last rays of sun set on another day. Enough that I had seen every variation of card shuffling celebration. More than once, I noticed, as I won yet another. Record time.

A couple hours ago Nate had come into the room and said, 'You know it's 3pm, right?'

I told him I did and he said, 'Well if you want anything from the kitchen you should probably get it now,' and closed the door.

His friends would be here at 6 to meet over croissants and talk about their screenplays. They came every Sunday at 6, and usually I was at the door to greet them and lead them to their pain au chocolat, their honey glazed, flaky pastry and jam, which they would pick over just as meticulously as they did their spec scripts. But lately Nate and I had come to an unspoken agreement that we would pretend I wasn't home. It wasn't very hard to do.

I looked out the window and saw a woman bent over a patch in her garden, overalls hanging on her slim body, her blonde hair in a messy bun, trimming leaves or pulling weeds — I couldn't tell from up here. We lived in an apartment building on the outskirts of LA, far enough out that it had another name altogether. Looking at the woman I thought I might be happier if I had a yard. A door I could open to go outside, instead of having to climb down four flights of stairs, walk through the lobby past Shelia—whose job it seemed to be to sit in front of the elevator and complain to anyone who walked by that it was broken — out the front door, just to stand around the corner, hands jutting into my pockets, until a catcaller made me nervous and I went back up.

A man walked out of the house and joined the woman in the yard; I saw him put his arms around her and they looked very peaceful in the purple light of the evening.

For a moment I wanted to be the type of woman who gardened. Who dug in the dirt and planted my bulbs, bulbs I'd picked from the local farmer's market where I went every Sunday with a man — my boyfriend — who had a beard and wore flannel shirts, and spoke earnestly about soil. And at night we would make tea with those big seeds and watch them bloom, and in bed we'd make quiet, gentle love. His kisses would taste like the earth. And that's all that would matter to me, my garden and his love.

I heard people coming in, Nate's laugh in the hallway just outside the door, and I turned away from the window as the couple walked back into their house, already feeling like it wouldn't be enough.

A month or two ago Nate told me he couldn't move to New York when I graduated at the end of the year, that it was too late in his career to be making that kind of change. He asked me if it was OK and I said yes, even though I felt like I'd been cracked open and hollowed out when he said it, his eyes nervously watching for my reaction, but words steady and convinced, like he knew better.

I guess that was the problem: he always acted like he knew better. He said he'd wanted to live in New York when he was

21, too. I guess it bugged me, him always acting like what I was feeling was nothing new.

I fell back onto the pillow and looked across the room at my dresser. It didn't start then, all this. It'd been building, really. From I don't know what. It just felt like weight.

In New York, I wouldn't feel that weight. In New York I'd be the type of woman who hangs out in speakeasies and goes to art galleries. I'd live in a loft in Manhattan and have cocktails with my theater friends. I'd be surrounded by an undeniable energy. I'd be much better there.

I dragged myself off of the bed, carrying the weight on my shoulders and neck, and took my suitcase from out of the closet. I packed quietly, there were only clothes, everything else was his. I listened to the muffled sounds of the group in the living room, tried to discern Nate's professorial timbre, to hear if there was any shaky recognition in his voice.

Two years ago we'd sat in his car outside my residence hall, in the back of the parking lot where no one would see us, and he told me it wouldn't work. He told me we were at two different points in our lives and that I was going to change and he wasn't.

I said he could convince himself, but he wasn't going to convince me.

Now I waited for the last of his group to leave and when I was sure everyone was gone I walked into the living room with my suitcase. All of the croissants were gone, the plate was sticky and dusted with crumbs. He nodded slowly and said, OK. We looked at each other and the inevitability of it all hurt worse than anything.

CLEANLINESS IS NEXT
TO GODLINESS
Srishti Chaudhary

It was as if Goddess Lakshmi herself had walked through their doors the day Esha got employed. And why not? Her mother saved a little bit every day to buy and keep a single marigold in front of the small idol they were given by the couple whose house she cleaned, and so it was only fair that their prayers were answered. To be fair, this wasn't what she originally wanted for Esha; she was a growing girl and it was better that she be married off than give others a chance to bring untoward looks towards her. But this was an offer they could not refuse. The local British office at the *paanch-batti chowk* in Jaipur had offered Esha the chance to sweep their office, and gave her three rupees a month in return.

Esha got off to a good start; she arrived on time every day, 6.30 am, as they had asked her, and swept and cleaned until 9. They liked her work – she did not speak until spoken to, was almost invisible to the people in the office and did not ask unnecessary questions. She would knock on the door in the morning, whip her hands in a 'namastey' while bowing her head, and go straight towards the broom, which always lay next to a wall sign which said, 'Cleanliness is next to Godliness'. She never asked for water herself, and only drank it when the office warden would insist. Esha was not stupid; she knew that drinking the water from the cup of any higher caste Hindu would get her into a lot of trouble. But the white people didn't seem to mind, so she chanced it once, and then did it again.

She would use the broom to sweep away all the dirt that came in stuck to the soles of the *sahibs'* leather shoes. She did it slowly but effectively, sweeping around in a way that she was almost not a presence, but only like the light wind that would come in through the windows sometimes and move the curtains. Once everything was swept off, she would use an old, damp cloth to make sure that the surface of the floor would shine. If someone were to walk over her newly cleaned floor, she never complained, but wiped it clean once more.

After a few weeks of working there, they asked Esha to stay there throughout the day so as to help them run things smoothly in the office. Her role would involve serving tea, food, cleaning the floor, dusting the tables, washing the dishes, and running an errand here and there if need be. They offered her eight rupees in return; it was more money than her entire family earned in total.

So Esha left at six in the morning, taking the longer route as she was not allowed to walk through the special lanes of the upper-castes, and spent the whole day, cleaning and pruning, washing and drying, making sure everything was as smooth and clean as they liked it to be. Now she spent a lot more time in the company of the *sahibs*, and realised that they spoke to each other in Hindi sometimes, for practice. She listened quietly as they rehearsed their broken Hindi, and deeming the girl to be a harmless, sweet, little thing, asked her to correct them if they said something wrong. Esha at first blushed and shook her head, not wanting to prove the *sahibs* wrong, but slowly gave in and corrected their tenses and verbs.

She listened as they talked about the Major's visit in the coming month, and debated Gandhi's arrest; she heard as they mused about the weather back home and cursed Jaipur's sun. One amongst them, James Brown, or Captain James Brown as some seemed to refer to him, was particularly vocal in his opinions about the Indian people. Esha heard as he claimed that there was something inherently dirty about them and that they were not to be trusted in any matter. If Captain James Brown was to begin one of his tirades when she was present, someone else on his behalf would give her anxious glances; but what would she know? Esha was as invisible as the wind, after all.

Captain James Brown, then, would then, have no qualms about stating his express opinion when it came to colonized Indians. 'Each is worse than the other, dirt and scum of the world,' he'd say, taking a deep swig of his evening tea, 'little scoundrels. But who knows if there is some truth in what they say? Maybe the lower castes are even worse; I wouldn't touch them with a six-foot flagpole.' Captain Brown, then, would ask Esha to always wash her hands with the soap he especially purchased before she served him; he would ask her to hold out her hands and show them to him so he could be assured of their cleanliness. And so Esha would do as he said, never judging, never complaining, only going about her job as she was told to, just sometimes gritting her teeth, sometimes pursing her lips. She went about her day as required, obeying, not aspiring.

It was one of the busy days at the office, as everybody prepared for the visit of the Major due the next day. Esha had to work extra hard and clean twice as much, as they emptied drawers full of trash, strewn away instead of thrown; all the paintings were taken down and cleaned, and Esha had to keep a step-stool on the top of the chairs to reach the vent which had to be made free of spider webs. She rubbed the bathrooms squeaky clean, making sure everything shone, for it was the way she was taught at home, to never leave a trace of dirt if she could see it.

Captain Brown was in a particularly bad mood and grumbled all over; he berated Mrs. Williams, the secretary, for not archiving the paperwork and walked up and down the hall, attacking anyone who came in the way and finally calling for a meeting to discuss tomorrow's program. They decided they would welcome the Mayor with flowers, lead him to breakfast in the office, and then take him for a short city tour and finally coming back to office after lunch to discuss administrative matters. Captain Brown insisted that Esha and all other temporary Indian servants were to be neatly dressed with aprons and try to appear in front of the Mayor as little as possible.

It was ten past five in the evening soon and with a scramble of the chairs, the crowd began to disperse. Esha waited in a corner as Captain Brown received a phone call and spoke with nonchalance. She looked around as they picked up their briefcases, chatting on their way out, and gave Captain Brown a brief, nervous look which turned into a wave of goodbye.

Captain Brown turned around, waving his hand in impatience, and got immersed in his phone call. Esha watched him as he scratched his nose, then put one finger inside and rotated. His finger swept the inside of his nose, slowly and thoroughly; when the finger was withdrawn, it had on its tip phlegm mixed with grime, which he examined with a distracted eye and then wiped it on the table. He repeated the action several more times until he was sure nothing bothered his nose anymore, and was about to reach for the jar of biscuits on his table when he noticed Esha watching him.

He gave her a hasty smile, as if she had caught him in the act; she didn't return the smile. She stared at him as he went back to his phone call and pretended to be very busy. She looked at him as he walked to the end of the room to the table, pacing impatiently and scratching his head. He glanced at her a few times, thinking that would make her look away but Esha looked on at him.

Finally, he hung up the phone and gave Esha a hardened, condescending look, daring her to say something, willing her to speak. She stared at him calmly, and once Captain Brown was assured that the matter was settled, he walked away with carefully measured footsteps.

She stared at his desk, imagining for one mad moment how it would be if she could just walk away. How it would be if she just walked away from this dirty desk, into the busy street, towards the sunset. How it would be if she could just keep walking as long her legs would run. Would she reach the end, would she touch the horizon? But then she looked at the grime stuck on the desk, folded her soap-washed hands together, and walked towards the mop that lay in the corner.

FRANKIE

Zoe McMillin

The ferry shudders under Agatha's feet. She always needs the detox of ocean wind after going to the mainland. Crofton to Campbell River, all for a damn dog. Their old Honda followed logging trucks the majority of the way up highway 19. She looks back at the car where Ryan is asleep behind the wheel. She can see the edge of the blanket their son is curled up under in the back seat. The dog lies warm in her arms, nose twitching along the current the ferry whips up. He is an Irish setter, 10 weeks old, a russet sleek ball of fur and sharp teeth. He tires out craning his head for seagull smells and rests his jaw against her forearm. The breeder told her to hold him to lessen the anxiety of separation. He sighs and shuts his eyes. The hair on the top of his head tufts up into a mohawk in the breeze.

It is like having a baby again. It is like all that maternal fear is returning. She is going to be this dog's mother. She is going to use this dog to fix things.

Agatha got married in 1989. Her mother got sick in 1995, two years after Agatha's son was born. Mama was a stylish woman, a little out of place in the west coast woods. She always wore bright red lipstick. She sat cross-legged in chairs and gestured with her hands as she spoke, and listened with intense concentration to her grandson's chattering. She made tea with the milk in first, an exact half-inch at the bottom of the cup. She was fine, at first. She took walks and drove and behaved like a retiree. Then Mama forgot her car keys in the library, or couldn't unlock her bike, or left the stove on. She talked about the past, how the outside of her house was yellow when she was a child, so when she moved in Ryan painted their kitchen walls bright as egg yolks. In living with her again, Agatha found out that Mama was seasonally depressed, and that it made her obsessed with light. Their house had large windows, but Mama's room was full of lamps, recessed ceiling lights, emergency flashlights by the bed and in the side table drawer. Agatha would wake up to the slamming of that drawer at night, and knew Mama was getting up, twisting the small metal flashlight on, and finding her way to the bathroom by its weak beam.

Three Christmases passed with Mama's dementia. Today was New Year's Eve 1999. Mama's room hadn't been occupied since November, but all her things were still in there. Turkey sat in the freezer, next to half a bag of brussels sprouts because Mama used to love them but by her last Christmas they were left on her plate in an oil slick of gravy.

They had sat with paper crowns and candles, and Mama said, *switch with me Ryan, purple's not your colour*, and gave her son-in-law the green crown sagging on her own head. He helped adjust the purple one over her thin white hair, and she smiled for the rest of the evening. She clapped at her grandson's poem recital.

Get this boy a pet, she said.

Mama dictated, and people obeyed. Research ensued. Google got filled with searches for 'sporting dogs', 'dogs good with children', 'breeders close by'.

That morning, New Year's Eve 1999, Agatha had looked out the french window at the back yard and remembered their

117

appointment.

'You gotta strike the match away from you, buddy,' Ryan said behind her. He held a packet of Redbird matches in his hand and crouched in front of the wood stove with their son in the crook of his elbow, scraping match on box to make a flame.

'Not working!' their son cried, and bent down to crumple more newspaper in his hands.

'It will, you just have to try again. Come here,' Ryan said.

This Christmas right after Mama's death, Agatha's head hadn't been entirely together, to say the least. She hadn't felt the will to clean out Mama's room. The one thing she resolved to keep was her bicycle, out in the woodshed covered in a tarp. It could be nice to ride that bicycle into town, once summer came. So, with all her thoughts on the holidays sobered by her thoughts on how to pack away her mother's life, she forgot about the breeder's appointment until that morning.

'No!'

'Light the paper first.'

'No, Dad!'

You made a mistake, Mama used to say, *falling in love with a woodsman*.

Agatha made no mistake at all. Ryan built their house. A tiny house, on the edge of a dried-out, rocky arbutus grove. It had a wide front porch, where their son leaned over the side and spat and you'd never see where it landed, it went so far down the bluff. The first thing Agatha did on moving in was put wind chimes by the front door. In the early construction days of framing and tarps, she remembered catching lizards on the sun-hot kitchen tile who would drop their tails. Later, she remembered Mama wandering in her dressing robe, black with cranes flying over the back that looked animated when she moved, and how she always stood in a sunbeam for a few seconds, wiggling her toes. *I like the warmth*, she said. *It's good for arthritis*.

The ferry propellors change pace and the dog lifts its head again.

Agatha keeps her eyes on the skyline, where day is fading into pink over the island's trees, and the boat slows as it comes into the little harbour of Vesuvius Bay. She walks back to the car.

They dock, and engines start. The dog doesn't like the metal clatter of cars leaving the rampart. He whines. Agatha keeps him in her lap, stroking the top of his head as he twitches back and forth. He barks and puts his front paws on the dashboard.

'No!' she says, tugging him away. Ryan laughs.

She dozes on the drive. At home, Ryan carries the child, she carries the dog. Ryan puts the boy to bed and she goes through the house and turns on all the lights, and the radio on low too. Frank Sinatra is playing. She sits on the floorboards and lets the dog lick her palm. He sniffs her clothes, puts his paws on her chest to reach her face. Sniffing, sniffing. His breath hits her own sense of smell and she wrinkles her nose. She hears Ryan in his heavy boots going back down the hall and outside.

The puppy's head snaps around as the car doors slam. Ryan comes back in holding the dog crate.

'What are we naming him?' he says, setting it down.

Agatha strokes the dog's ears. 'He doesn't need a name yet.' The dog licks her chin. 'Do you?' she says. She hugs around his little ribs. 'Do you, pup?'

He wriggles from her grip and scampers at Ryan's feet.

'Frankie?' Ryan kneels down. 'Our new millennium dog, huh?' The dog sits. His tail wags. Agatha watches Ryan's palm smooth down the dog's back, again, again.

THE SPOT

James J. Valliere

There it is, above my bed. The spot. It's been there since you left. At the beginning, it was no bigger than a thumbtack, and now it's the size of a softball. The spot is an oozing sponge-like mass of vile reddish purple, insidious in its design. Thin veins of its material are spreading, peeling the soft white paint and cracking the walls. In the centre, the spot is heaving, a corrosive slime moving up and down. Up and down.

I wonder if this is my imagination…a hallucination.

The spot has been here so long that I've begun to think that there has never been a time without it. The memories are fuzzy, dusty fragments flittering around my frantic thoughts. Nights are the worst. I am fixated by thoughts of the spot and that is when these dreadfully happy memories of spotless days are clearest.

Perfect walls, no spot. Your first time sleeping over. After hours of me tossing and turning, afraid you'll tire of me soon enough, that it's too good to last, I allow myself to fall asleep in your arms. My head on your chest, following the rhythm of your breaths, letting the scent of your skin consume me. You smell like orange-zest freshly grated in preparation of making pan de los muertos *and flour spilled over a shirt fresh from the dryer. You smell safe.*

In the morning, when I wake, finding myself still in your arms, you pulling me tighter, my back pressing into your chest, you kiss me on the back of my neck, whispering, 'Good morning.'

It's these days, the days before the spot, that I cling to. The more I do, the more the spot seems to grow.

I lay in bed. My side, of course, not yours. The spot is the size of a large dog now. Its tentacle arms have broken from the walls and are spreading across the floor. I should stop thinking of you. I don't know how. Not when you're the clearest reference point of pre-spot days.

We're in the kitchen. Making breakfast. You give me one job. A simple job. I turn the sausages while you do everything else, not saying a word, watching me from the corner of your eye, humming the tune of an old Johnny Cash song.

Afterwards, we stretch out in your bed, feeling gross and heavy and warm and content. You play with my hair, twirling it in your fingers, teasing me that it smells like rubber gloves and baby powder. I try to object, and you launch your assault, tickling me so that my entire body flails about. I nearly fall off the bed, but you catch me, saving me just before I plummet. You stare at me in complete silence.

It's in this moment, I take a deep breath and reveal myself. I am shaking, nervously rubbing your chest as I confess what we both feel. You kiss me, tell me not to worry, assure me I'll be okay, that this will turn out okay. That we'll be okay.

I wonder if the shattering of that promise is what has brought the spot.

Slimy vines are dropping off the ceiling. They are winding and

121

curling, making a thick jungle inside the room. Strange bottle-green buds have begun to appear. A massive one is splintering the heart of the spot. The twisting arms of the spot sprawl forth, slewing about on what was once your side, outlining a missing shape. It lingers for a moment, taunting me with your shadow, until the spot's hunger forces it to continue to consume. All that is left is my place on the bed.

We find ourselves in your bed. Again. This time, it is you cuddling up to me, your back pressing against my chest. You're breathing steadily. Side to side, we watch some silly Kung Fu movie poorly dubbed.

In it, I find nothing, except your happiness. I run my fingers delicately across your neck; inhale your scent, feel your body rise and expand as you laugh, finding joy, and in that I find it too. It is enough to see your serious face break, revealing a hidden and infectious laugh. It is worth it to feel your happiness ripple through your body and then outwards, filling the room. It makes the movie enjoyable to experience your carefully guarded peace. I envelop myself in it, feeling the warmth of your most treasured secret, and I kiss the top of your head.

After the movie, we lie in your bed, on our sides, face-to-face. You are nearly asleep, the rhythm of your breathing slower.

And I panic. Doubt. I know it, you know it, and sooner than later it will be ripped from my hands and I will no longer feel the warmth of your secret laugh or smell your orange-zest. It will be forever gone and I will be left with nothing but faded memories of something intangible. Better now to cut and run, to get out while I still can.

And so I make my move. I start to pull back, mumble how I should get going. That I have to be up early the next day. I am nearly gone, but you reach and pull me closer, whispering, 'Stay, at least for a little longer.'

And so I did, unlike you, who, when I asked you to stay, you left.

I have written you into mythology. You're even farther out of reach by my placing you in the stars. I can look up in wonder, trying to connect the dots but the order escapes me. Each remembering, each retelling, I arrange you slightly differently. In some versions, you are the gallant hero, and in others, I cast you as a villain in a narrative long since over. It has become impossible to know the truth when each time the story changes. And the more I try to put these fragments of something back together, the more the spot grows, the more it devours, leaving me with nothing.

The spot traces the outline of my body. Ropes of thick green vines move across me, binding me to this place in the room. I watch the massive sprout in the centre of the spot. It is starting to bloom.

Orange and white flowers reveal themselves, filling the room with your dangerous scent. All the flowers are awake now, in full bloom, their hateful beauty on display, and all I can breathe, all that I can smell, all that I can taste, and feel, and know, is the memory of you.

EXCERPTS

The Plant Delivery Man
An Excerpt

Caitlin Malone McLaughlin

My mum still tries to convince me that I made him up. Apparently, I was a lonely child, prone to starting conversations with myself. What I now keep carefully hidden from her is that I'm a lonely adult, still prone to conversing with myself. I can be found muttering in supermarket aisles, at the office, or in the car as I run my errands. I have learned to carefully conceal these exchanges by reducing them to barely audible mumbles that could almost be mistaken for the melodious hum of someone in a casually contemplative state. Not someone neurotically debating whether or not a grown woman can justify paying five pounds for a box of Lucky Charms.

The conversations I had as a child, however, weren't murmured. They were performed, often to my anatomically correct squid plushy, a result of that trip to the aquarium I took when I was four. I would create elaborate narratives about Brixton The Squid and our various pirate expeditions. So, it's understandable that my mum didn't believe me when I told her about The Plant Delivery Man.

I still don't know his name. Not really. I asked him the day we met. He told me it wasn't important. That I should concern myself with learning the names of the plants instead.

'They can be rather troublesome to articulate.'

I didn't know what that meant, but I nodded, because he was an adult and presumably attempting to impart wisdom.

The Plant Delivery Man could never be captured in a name, anyway. Now, when I think of him, instead of a name, I hear the crumble of rubber wheels on the dirt path that led to our porch. He pedals an odd contraption, a cross between a bicycle and an enormous radio flyer wagon. The entire device is painted the same happy green that can be found inside an avocado. He drives using large handlebars that a small wicker basket hangs from. That's where he kept my delivery on the day I met him.

I had been playing in the front garden with Brixton. I heard an odd clatter as he approached, and I looked up. At six years old, I was still in the phase of childhood in which the strangeness of the world is constantly apparent, and one cannot fully distinguish the odd from the acceptable. So I appraised him with the same amount of curiosity I'd been devoting to a rotund snail shell just seconds before.

He was tall. Well, most people were tall to me at that age, but he seemed taller than normal. His limbs looked too long, all folded up against the pedals like the collapsible metal piping my mum had used to set up the tent on our family camping trips. He pedaled leisurely, trailed by what I discovered was the sound of clay pots rattling against tin. Instead of following the uneven brick path up to the doorway, he pedaled onto the grass and met me in the garden. I was reluctant to approach him. He was a stranger, and I had explicitly promised my mother *not* to converse with those.

But, he was in the garden and doing that thing that adults sometimes do where they lower themselves to be eyelevel with you, abolishing any implication of seniority. He reached into the

126

wicker basket that hung between those tusk-like handle bars and removed a white ceramic pot with delicate etchings that reminded me of eyelet lace.

'Who are you?' I asked

'Helianthus annuus.' His voice was husky and grumbled out like woodchips.

'That's an odd name,' I thought out loud.

'It's not mine. It belongs to this guy,' he said, setting the pot in front of me.

'That's a pot of dirt,' I said, forgetting my nerves.

'Are you sure?'

'It looks like a pot of dirt.'

'Well, why don't you hold on to Helianthus annuus for me, and see what happens to this pot of dirt with a little care.' He gave simple instructions for its care and promised to return when it first flowered. Then he departed with a wink on his strange metal contraption. I was young and lacking an attention span for many things, but this kind stranger's blind faith in me drove me to follow his instructions meticulously.

As directed, I watered the pot and sat it on my well-lit windowsill. I sang to it before I went to sleep and whispered praise to it in the morning. Sometimes, I even read it bedtime stories. That last one was not mandated, but as waxy, green leaves began to sprout from the soil, I felt overcome with the pride of imbuing life, and I was determined to love my creation, not just care for it. Plus, I was curious to see what would eventually bloom.

I woke one morning to the sound of rubber tires grasping at my driveway. I rubbed my eyes and discovered, at the top of what had become a stalky stem, the crowning bulb had unfurled, revealing the saffron petals of a sunflower. I peered past my beautiful creation, out the window, and saw the top of a straw hat as The Plant Delivery Man stood on the porch. I snatched the pot and ran to meet him.

'Helianthus annuus,' I stated proudly.

'He is indeed.'

'Are you here to take him away?'

'No, darling, he's yours, now. You must take care of him.'

And I did. I watched him grow and bloom and wilt, until withered petals, like clumps of scraggly blonde hair, fell from the head to litter my windowsill. Then I plucked up the remnants of the seeds, repotted him just as I'd been instructed, and started the process all over again.

This time, the sun-dipped petals were not a surprise but a much anticipated success. The morning my seed flowered, I snatched the pot and ran to the porch. I waited, shivering slightly in my lemon patterned pajamas as I peered through the early morning fog. The sun was still making its way over the horizon. My ears strained to hear the familiar chorus of his delivery vehicle. But the air remained still and quiet. Eventually, my mother came to collect me. We argued briefly about my being shoeless and out in the cold, awaiting what, to my mother, was an imaginary friend. I returned to my room and debated neglecting the little creature as a testament to my disappointment.

I placed it back on the windowsill. In preventing the sun from bleaching it, the pot had left a ring of slightly darker wood on the ledge, so I always knew just where to set my plant. The fog had started to clear, and the honeycomb light of dawn was seeping into the room, setting the petals aglow. I brushed my fingertips against their delicate, silky surface with the gesture my mother used to move hair from my face. Brixton The Squid was sitting in his spot on the opposite end of the sill. His tentacles were splayed out, pointing in my plant's direction, nothing but backlit dust particles dancing between them. I realized in that moment that both were precious to me. I walked to my ivory coloured bookshelf and selected Kevin Henke's *Chrysanthemum*, my bedtime story from the previous night. I settled onto the carpet below my friends and began reading to them in the window-light, all thoughts of defiant neglect forgotten.

No Lights in the Transoms
An Excerpt

Jessica Irish

She squeals for me in the night, and midday, and when the house is shaking with thunder, and when it's otherwise so quiet I can hear my own death reaching for me with spindly hands. She screams and I hold her to my chest, begging her to be quiet while her face turns purple from yowling.

On days when there is no strength left within me, Isaac fills the void. He heaves himself up from the floor and finds her in the cradle he's crafted for her out of old crates, tucks her under his chin and murmurs sweet secrets to her about a world she'll never know. He sings her the folk songs he wrote long ago, about people who got many chances to live good lives, and lost them all. Sometimes she quiets. Sometimes it grows worse.

She suckles at my breasts and I pray that I have enough nutrients within me to pass along to her. I can't look at her, can't acknowledge the mess we're in, but I also don't want to blame her for the pain she causes me, the cracked skin around my nipples, the heaviness of my body. I'm still recovering from the damage she's wrought in me. I know it's not her fault but I avoid looking at her all the same, because the other things I could blame – Oliver, fate, the disease that didn't take me – are not present for me to punish. So I look away from her while she feeds. I stare at the spackle that swirls in inorganic patterns on the wall and ignore the weight of her small body in my arms.

Every week we eat less; now Isaac and I are splitting just one can of soup a day. I'm always thirsty. We can't go outside, the sky is too damaged now. We stay sealed up in our house, hoping that our air will last, but it's a dull hope because I have no effort left to spend on the future. My head always aches. I dream about the scent of coffee, the feel of a warm mug in my hands.

Isaac and I sleep curled up with each other every night. He smells of salt, dried plums, and smoke, all mixed with something ranker: the worst the body can do when left to its own devices, unaided by water and soap.

He wraps his arms around me and pulls me close to him, and I'm not sure what our rules are now, but I know that there is some warmth between us when we do this, so I allow it, I sink into it. When she's in a particularly chaotic mood, I let him take her from her repurposed crates and set her softly between us on our blankets.

It's not what family ever looked like in my imagination.

'She needs a name, Nees,' he says to me.

It's morning and the sheets are tangled up around my leg. Everything is sweaty, my skin itches from it. She's gurgling and he's hovering over her, offering a finger to her. She wraps her little left hand around it and smiles up at him.

'Mmph,' I say, throwing an arm over my face.

'It's not right,' he says. 'It's almost been a month.'

I roll onto my side, squint at them.

'Pick something,' I say. 'You decide.'

'No,' he says. He raises himself up so he's sitting and crosses his legs. 'It's not for me to do that.'

I prop myself up on my elbows, look at her.

I haven't been able to name her, because for the longest time I didn't believe I'd made something real.

The first week, I was certain she would die. I knew that I was on the brink as well; I figured that one of us would pave the way for the other. Our breathing just a succession of slow, half-hearted *puffs* until it ceased completely, leaving Isaac to survive on his own. Which he would, which was always his specialty.

Isaac called her *Sweet Pea*, and *Little Darlin'*, and he watched me with narrowed eyes, opening his mouth to speak, closing it again when he caught the darkness flashing in my eyes.

The second week, she got stronger, louder. I got more tired.

The third week, we collapsed into this routine, this slurping of soup, this praying for solace. It was easier then to continue; it's all I know how to do now.

And here we are, still alive in spite of the air, and still here in front of me is this creature who's learning what it means to be anything at all.

'I'm gonna cook some breakfast,' Isaac says, though we stopped eating breakfast three months ago. 'I think it's time for a real meal. You need to eat something, Anise. You've got to get back to fighting. And you have to name this baby.'

He doesn't wait for me to respond; he gets up and moves to the kitchen. I hear the dishes clanking, the propane lighting. I imagine what the meal could possibly be: probably Spam, or some other canned meat. Whatever it is, it smells good.

The baby stretches her arms out and makes a noise like a kitten. She has pretty, soft eyelashes and a head full of curly black hair. We don't look related, she has Oliver's nose. She's already prettier than I'll ever be.

Isaac still thinks he'll find Oliver, still believes that he's waiting for us in some field, some meadow, maybe in the cavern that now exists where we once pitched our tents. I don't know what he thinks he knows about Oliver, what has him believing it's important to find him. *I* know the facts, which are simple: this baby would not be a blessing to him. And: he would not love me more, not love me at all, because of her.

I reach out a finger and stroke her hair. She stares at me with the widest of eyes.

'who are you,little i?' I whisper to her, from a poem I'm surprised I remember. Neither of us blink. The current running between us feels like strength.

I snap us out of it first, press my hands into the floor and lift myself up. I bend down for her, place her back in her crib, stars swimming in front of my face because I've gotten up too fast. She mewls at me again and I shush her the way I think a good mother might. She closes her eyes and I turn away.

I move to the kitchen, watch Isaac toasting hot dogs right over the open flame of the camp stove. Three of them already sit on a plate, sweating with grease and smoking from heat. He burns his finger on the one he's cooking; he drops it onto the plate and sucks in air, shakes out his hand.

'Damn,' he says, turning to acknowledge me. 'That was stupid.'

I manage a thin smile. I know he can see the sadness in it.

He licks his finger, nods towards the plate of dogs.

'Smell good, don't they?' he says.

'They do,' I say. I come over to the table and sit down. He's rooting through the cabinet, pulling out mustards, offering me a variety. 'Isaac.'

'Yeah?' he says, glancing behind me, towards the living room where she's lying, sleeping.

'I can't name her because I don't know how.'

No Lights in the Transoms

He sits down next to me, props his chin in his hand.

'Okay,' he says. 'I get that.'

Tension flows out of my body, my shoulders roll back.

'You do?' I say.

'Sure,' he says. 'But it's bullshit.'

'What?'

'You're freaked, you think we're doomed. But the kid needs a name, Nees. She's alive. She's living.'

'For how long?' I whisper.

'Doesn't matter,' he says.

'If I name her,' I say. 'If I name her, and I lose her, you will have to kill me.'

He swallows, staring at me. Flicks his eyes up and down my face, deciding, I think, if it's something he can promise.

'Okay,' he says. 'I will.'

'Thank you,' I say.

'It's time,' he says. 'Do what needs doing.'

'You have to give me a minute,' I say. 'But I will.'

He nods, brings the plate in front of me. I pick up a hot dog, dip it in a new jar of grain mustard, and eat it in four bites. My stomach flips over with surprise, tightens. For a moment, I feel full.

'Maggie,' I say. 'Like your song.'

He hums the tune that seems to be her favourite, that calms her down more quickly than all the others. I don't remember all the words, but I try to sing along.

'Maggie,' he says. He nods, runs a hand through his beard. 'Let's go tell her.'

After Death
AN EXCERPT

Jacquelyn Chapman

I rode behind the armoured horsemen and watched as the bodies they dragged tore into dirt and dust, slowly, until there was nothing left but portions of bodiless heads. Any semblance of humanity had been scraped away and I wondered to which world their spirits had gone. All that was left here were raw, fleshy-heaps that eventually fell off their tethers, leaving behind ropes that bounced to the rhythm of the horses to which they were attached. The knights leaned over and cut off the ropes with their swords, trying not to nick their horses in the process, glad to finally be rid of their burdens.

It was an hour until dusk and there was a slight drizzle in the air. The shadowed landscape whispered cryptic reflections of the wretched metropolis that lie ahead. We proceeded along a thinly trodden path over sedimentary rock through an endless valley, following a north-northwest line toward the city of Eidyn.

A one-year-old baby boy bounced on a thin pillow on the back of Lord Salrien's horse just ahead of me. The bird-like, metal cage that contained the babe stopped his tiny body from falling to the ground. Lord Salrien's cape, closer to a coal-black than the dark, forest green I knew it to be, draped over the child's cage on three sides, leaving the back unprotected and visible. My eyes bounced with the child's body, rattling in the cage like a toy.

The baby had long since learned that crying was useless. Crying did not get him what he wanted. What he wanted, what he needed, was his mother. But she was two horses ahead, mounted behind a knight, her hands tied together like a fugitive. A criminal. Our Maerié. Young Queen Maerié, with the warmth and kindness that even enemies had acknowledged in her eyes.

She had come willingly. Her forces met theirs—the Lords of our country (*her* country) had gathered their own troops—and Maerie conceded before any blood was shed. The terms of her capture was not information I was privy to as the newly appointed Counsel Priest. But I did know that they were taking the Queen and her child, the future King Jaimes, to Eidyn. I had no choice but to follow, or I would be the next body dismembered behind the horsemen.

They helped Maerie off her horse just outside the city walls at dusk. Her hands were still tied behind her as we made our way toward the city's center. It was a dirty city then. The stone buildings blackened with their aged wear. The stench of death and dying, of waste and the wasted, permeated every molecule of air.

The people of Eidyn stepped out of their homes as Lord Salrien paraded the tethered Queen through the High streets. Tapestry-like banners hung from every window along the march, billowing in the reeky wind. On each of them read one word: OVERTHRONE. They had known we were coming.

When we reached the top of the city, they placed Maerie underneath a Celtic cross on the north-side of the open grounds in front of the castle. The crowd formed around her. The people shouted and jeered. 'Over-throne! Over-throne!'

I remained just beyond the masses, watching helplessly, knowing I had no power or voice against the Lords, against this motley crew.

Maerie refused to look at anyone but her son, held in the hands of an armoured stranger, just out of her reach. She stood stoic and still, until the moment the knight lifted his blade to her son, and then she leapt. The knights held Maerie back as Lord Salrien stepped forward, having found her breaking point.

'Now, you will see the *new* future!' he cried. The crowd roared with excitement. Maerié's knees buckled.

Lord Salrien pulled out a scroll and let it dramatically unravel for the crowd. He then turned the document toward Maerié.

'Sign!' he called to her and forced a quill into her hand. He wanted her to abdicate the throne in favor of her son. The crowd echoed his demands.

Maerie looked at her baby, knife held to his tiny throat, and then back to the crowd. It was a cruel choice. Her son or her crown, she could only save one.

She drew in a breath and lifted her hand to the document. She signed her name on the scroll. MAERIE R.

I had just settled into the church below the castle when Lord Salrien paid me a visit shortly after the abdication. He entered my study with two knights trailing him like dogs, loyal or fearful of the power he held—maybe both.

'I shall accept your approval of my hand as ruling Regent of Eidyn,' he declared.

I hesitated. 'By... by what means do you come to this?'

Lord Salrien moved forward, two steps closer to me. 'It was always *this*.'

I started to back away, reaching for the little bit of courage I didn't know I had. 'Perhaps... perhaps you can tell me just what is going on here, my Lord.'

But I already knew. He had killed and dragged men to their

bones, captured and forced the Queen to relinquish her throne, so that he, Lord Salrien, could become ruler, Regent for the one-year-old King Jaimes.

Lord Salrien looked back at his knights with a slight nod of his head and the three of them drew their swords in unison. I fluttered toward the wall.

Lord Salrien bent his elbow back, sword in hand, and took a slice across my neck.

I flew out of my body quickly through the laceration in my throat. There was no longer a third dimensional version of me — the body of the priest I had been was dead. But I was not gone.

I looked up to notice I was still in the study of the cathedral in Eidyn. The mortal knights had dragged my former body out and a single human servant now cleaned up the blood. He did not notice me. And I remembered... humans couldn't see spirits.

A deep, belly laugh came from inside the room and I realised that three men with familiar grins stared at me from the far corner. I knew they were not mortal.

'Looks like you've just been womped on the head,' laughed the pudgy one in a saffron robe. A flash of a lifetime I had spent with him in a temple, high in the mountains of Shaoshi, blinked before me — like I had flipped through a book and retained all the information it held.

'Don't worry, shouldn't take but a second more for it to all come back to you,' said the one dressed in a white vestment and fishtail-shaped hat. Again, a lifetime flickered through me, of he and I as devote priests of Vatican City.

'Better?' asked the third one, a large Mongolian warrior with a thin, pointed moustache. I had fought beside him in the Battle of Ain Jalut, long ago.

'I... I couldn't help,' I stammered.

'You can, if you still want,' said the Vatican priest.

'But not alone,' spoke the monk in a serious tone.

The Vatican priest spread his arms out toward the city of Eidyn. 'Gather others who have similar ties to this part of the mortal realm.'

'You know one already,' continued the monk.

'Go to her,' commanded the warrior. 'Guide her.'

So I went back to the mortal world. But not as a human. And not as a spirit. This time, I went back as a bird.

I went to the day she would die, a mere fortnight after I had seen her last, when I was a priest and she was a Queen abdicating her throne. A crowd gathered as it had before, in the same open grounds outside the castle. But now, in front of the Celtic cross, stood a block and an axe.

Maerie walked out of a shadowy side entrance as bells rang from high up in the castle walls. She wore a floor-length black cloak with a billowing hood. I could barely see more than the flush of her lips and the outline of her nose poking through the cape's shadow. The leather shoes on her feet twisted at the tips like handles to a cane. Hell was in the minds of the people in the crowd as they pointed fingers that may as well have been knives.

I decided to show myself to Maerie when she reached the cross. I appeared as a wren, a sweet, light-colored bird rarely seen in the city of Eidyn. I fluttered toward her as she lay her head on the block. Her eyes grasped mine and mine grasped hers. Then she smiled.

'Into thy hands, I commend my spirit,' she whispered. My message had been received. She knew she was not alone.

And then, the blade came down.

Nothing Lies Beyond
AN EXCERPT

Vassilena Parashkevova

Of bodies changed to other forms I tell ...
Ovid, *Metamorphoses*

I.

'Last night I woke up standing,' I said.

Dr. Ben Sussum's eyes returned to me, ripped from a placid daydream still reflected in them, blinked and readjusted focus. He suffered from some rare eyelid condition that made him look, at best, hung-over and, at worst, savaged by dogs. In the eyes, at least, and their raw, skin-graft-like lids. I wondered if it hurt him to blink.

'Go on,' he said and sat up.

'I . . . I knew I was awake, but my eyes were closed and I wondered why I couldn't see. When I opened them, I still couldn't make anything out. I could only hear the pulse in my temples. I started groping my way round but objects felt strange, someone else's. The door was not where it was supposed to be. I tripped over something massive with a sharp edge that caught my knee as I fell forwards. I headed back, with …'

He started rolling his pen between thumb and forefinger.

'… with my arms stretched out in front of me, like a zombie. And I started reasoning, feverishly reasoning. Running places in my mind that could have been the world around me. Till my hand met a familiar shape.'

I looked at his pen. He stopped rolling it.

'Yeees?' he said.

'I felt the object. It was heart-shaped. I knew immediately where I was and how I'd got there.'

'And where were you?'

'Here. In my room.'

'With the heart-shaped object? I assume it's not *your* heart?' Eyebrows arching, patchwork eyelids at full spread, he took a matter-of-fact sip of coffee in slow motion.

'A spare one maybe. It's a box, a jewellery box. One I never liked, though.'

'Why not?'

'It's cheap, kitschy; its varnish has peeled off in places. The colours are ugly: dark green, brownish streaks. Leaves, they're meant to be. It's supposed to be an imitation of a vaguely Eastern style – Chinese maybe, or Mongolian. But it's plastic and, well, heart-shaped. Might as well have kittens painted on it. Kittens and roses.'

'How did you come to have this box?'

'I bought it or a friend did at the time, I can't remember.'

'And yet, it was so … significant in your dream?'

'I wasn't dreaming. I told you. I woke up and found myself standing.'

'At which point,' he raised his pen and pinned the point's location in the air, 'you saw the box and recognised it?'

'I didn't need to. I knew it with my hand.'

The pen noted something down. 'You're not wearing any jewellery now?'

'I didn't think it was a requirement. Besides, it clashes with the uniform, really.'

'Do you *wear* any jewellery? Here?'

'Sometimes. Mostly earrings. I like the way they clink and tinkle in the evening breeze as I stroll up and down the promenade. I'm sure they're delightful to the eye as well.'

'Whose eye?'

'The eye of the beholder.'

'How long have you been with us, Maya?'

'Here in paradise? A few weeks, maybe more, days merge.'

'Your English is very good, Maya.'

'So's yours, Dr. Sussum. You taught me language and my profit *on't* is I know how to curse.'

'I'm sorry?'

'Caliban. He was poorly taught. Still curses in Elizabethan English.'

'Oh, Caliban, I see,' he smiled. 'We've all done Shakespeare. Not much use for that here. Might even weigh you down.' He gave me a quick once-over. 'What brought you to our little island?'

'Fair winds and following seas. It was a natural progression, from one British island to another.'

'And why did you leave the first island?'

'Cannibalism.'

A frown. One second, two ... A smirk. No fool, Ben Sussum.

'The first island was full,' I explained, 'full to the brim with immigrants. Some were seen hanging on to the white cliffs of Dover with both hands. Dangling there, the silly beggars, above the English Channel. I was one of them and I let go.'

'So to speak?'

'If you wish.'

'Okay, thank you, Maya. Done some good work today, haven't we? Before you go – this is merely procedure – we expect everyone to write a few things in what we call their *metabio* diary. Feel free to write anything that comes to mind. Something you wish you'd shared with me, perhaps, but, for whatever reason, didn't? Couldn't? This is how we complete sessions. And, don't worry. It's confidential. Just you and me.'

'Who keeps this diary? You or me?'

'It will remain here, locked in this office. No one else will read it.'

Across the desk, he handed me a pencil and a sky-blue notebook that matched the colour of my uniform, with 'MAYA APOSTOLOVA' written in a cautious but determined hand on the cover. He leaned back in his chair, his gaze crawling up me to a point above my head.

'You have five minutes. Write until about quarter to.'

I heard the clock ticking on the wall behind me and instinctively looked at his wrist. No watch. How very unobtrusive! It's not me, I'm happy to be here. But there are rules larger than me that we all have to abide by, you'd agree? Time is my concern and you obstruct it.

I hovered over the page with the stubby little pencil. Not exactly inspiring confessional writing with this inferior instrument. Worn out with heavy use? No ink spilled.

It's a good thing I like blue, I wrote and looked up.

He made a few brisk hand circles to urge me to get on with it and looked out of the window. Outside, you've seen it all before. The ocean stretched, relentless, all the way to the horizon. And if you stared long and hard enough into the mirror-surfaced void, you'd see … no, not the Prime Meridian, but close. The 131st. As if we're on a ship, I thought, and promptly felt the floor pitch, then yaw. In a new line, I added:

And we did speak only to break the silence of the sea.

SOMEWHERE AND NOWHERE
AN EXCERPT

Zack Abrams

I want to find a place named Somewhere. It's out there. I can see it, bifurcated by a gargantuan and nameless body of water. The water has frozen on the falls. The moon refracts off the cascade and illuminates Somewhere all around it. There are no streetlights in Somewhere because the moon is always shining there. The people of Somewhere sleep during the day and then, in the night, they sing and chant and stomp their feet in immaculate three/ four time. I am floating out here. I am Nowhere.

The seats are cramped and the pilots are suicidal or tweaking. They spin us around; the wings dip and reach for the stratosphere. The seats shake like an old railcar in the turbulent thunderclouds. All around clouds lick each other with electric tongues. Water vapor streaks the window of the man next to me. He is nice. He seems to enjoy Nowhere. He has a flattering smile and addresses me as 'Sir.' His dark hair dances with static and laps against the window now as he looks out at Nowhere. He likes 'Red wine, whatever you have.' Ordered it just so three times. I like my scotch neat. The flight attendant gives me two miniature bottles each time. I think I've had six of them.

'Where are you headed?' His breath fogs the window so he wipes it away with his sleeve.

I say, 'Somewhere,' and he says to me,

'Oh, yah?'

'Yep. What about you?' I grab the evacuation card and flip through it.

'Boone. Then to Blowing Rock.'

'Driving?' I play with the latch to the seatback table.

'No. Sailing.' He laughs.

'Sailing down 421, eh? Where the hell is that drink cart; I'm going to get another, want one?'

He looks at me and says, 'Uh…yeah.'

'What do you want?'

'A Red, whatever they have.'

'Got it.'

I gaze into as many eyes as I can heading aft. In Nowhere, there is a mind behind each pair of eyes. To each pair of eyes – except for the fellow with the eye patch, I suppose – its own consciousness. How many of us hide our misery behind our many-colored irises? The plane rocks and drops. I fall into the lap of some sleeping child. Their mother pushes me into the aisle, and I mutter some apology. She is apoplectic, and I don't blame her.

'You two want a drink?' I say.

One of the lavatories says *Occupied* in large red letters. I pull on the door handle just to make sure. It holds fast. I nod my head as if that's all I wanted to know. I think that it was, but I'm not sure.

In Somewhere, they live in houses built and rebuilt throughout each age of man; singular homes that exist such as they exist nowhere else. Ranch and split-level, wood, brick, and stone. One concrete house and one made entirely of crystal, within which resides an irascible Dostoyevsky-obsessed pedagogue. There is always snow on the ground and the air is frigid.

A flight attendant rushes into the galley after me. It's too late, though. I've turned half a dozen cart drawers out and dumped them onto the floor. Cans of uninteresting drinks roll around and bang about on either side of the room as the pilots pitch us hither and thither. The attendant grabs hold of a cart to steady himself, but it comes loose and one of the drawers spews out and thuds against his cheek. His head smacks on the linoleum and the cart topples over onto his chest, sending bottles of spirits and wine across the floor. Seeing this, I scoop up as many as I'm able. Hearing the clack of unbuckling passengers, I slip into the vacant head and slide the latch. The toilet lid is up and, despite this, whatever slob before me missed that vast gaping blackness of the bowl entirely. My feet slip out from beneath me and my ass plunks into it.

I can see my reflection in the tiny window and it makes me laugh. Such as I am, I start stuffing the airplane bottles into my pockets, but for two Dewar's I suck down. My face is a red balloon. The image sends me into another convulsion.

'Sir?' My neighbor is banging on the door. I think it's him. It's too difficult to make out voices in here, though. 'Sir?' the voice says again.

'Hullo,' I call. Too loudly. Bells in my ears, now. I play with the latch, shake it about, 'the damn latch is stuck.' I say.

'Stuck, you say?'

'Stuck fast.' The words squeak through between laughter, half completed syllables split with snorts.

'Sir, are you okay?'

'I got your wine, friend. We're ready to go sailing.'

'So we are. Let's get you out of there, first.'

There is a place named Somewhere. I went as a child. I

have been searching for it my entire life. It comes to me most clearly, most vividly, when I am Nowhere. The lightning outside casts strobing lights on my hands. The faucet won't turn off. Nevertheless, I keep my hands beneath the stream and stare out the pitiful excuse of a window. The bathrooms all have bay windows and clawfoot tubs in Somewhere.

I remember now the banging on the door, the flight attendant in the galley.

'Sir. We need you to come out.'

'We?'

'We're worried about you.'

'Who's we?'

'Everyone. The crew, the passengers.'

'Oh.'

'Please come out. Can you get the latch to budge?'

'I'll give it another go.' He must be screaming. I can barely hear him. Nice fellow, though. Doing all this for me. I throw my weight against the latch, forgetting it was never stuck. The door slams open and I fall headlong, pants still around my ankles, into the cabin.

'Sorry, sorry!' I am always apologizing. A different flight attendant is helping me with my trousers. She seems harried and angry.

'Get your shit together, sir.' The galley is a mess of blood and food, but the other flight attendant is no longer underneath the trolley cart. I suppose there's always a silver lining. She carries me back to my seat. In Nowhere, even the best of us have overbearing guardians.

My neighbor is still looking out the window. His tray table is down in front of him with a new clear plastic goblet of wine. It's Red wine, whatever you got. He always gets it that way.

'They beat me to it,' I say.

'Beat you to what?' he says.

'Your order of Red wine, whatever you got. It's okay. I've brought more.' I rummage in my pockets and start stuffing liquor bottles into the seatback pocket.

'One sec, gotta dig through the dredge.'

He says, 'It's alright.' The lightning brightens the smile lines on his cheeks and I see dark stubble growing there. He is always smiling.

'Here,' I say.

I say, 'You know, I could have walked, but she wouldn't let me.'

'Happens to the best of us. Thanks for the Red, whatever it is. Cheers.' He turns to me and holds out his drink. I search for some scotch but the closest I come is cheap corn vodka.

'Cheers,' I say. Too loudly. People around us are staring, those who are still awake. In Nowhere, we sleep when we want, but we are rarely comfortable.

'Are planes conductors?' I say.

'No, planes are planes.' My neighbor says. He wipes the window with his sleeve.

'I mean, do they conduct electricity.'

'I believe each plane conducts its own orchestra.'

'So if we fly between two clouds, we could be struck by lightning, and all our electronics would get knocked out.'

'They only perform pieces by Strauss and Mendelssohn.'

'Perhaps it will shock us all, each at the same time. We will all fall into seizures simultaneously.'

'They avoid Opus 93, however. It is awful and should never be performed. *The Hebrides* is played in full, each flight.'

'I wonder, if we are over the sea, or over land, beneath these clouds. With us each in seizures, we'll be sure to crash. Unless the pilots are immune to electric shock. I suppose that explains our current flight path.'

'*Metamorphosen* follows *The Hebrides* with Goethe's poem read in accompaniment. Both the journals and diaries of Mendelssohn and Strauss are made available to each passenger upon request. They hope it inspires another cultural revolution.'

'I am certain our pilots are suicidal.'

My neighbor turns to me now. 'Suicidal?'

'You must know.'

'Know what?'

'The statistics?'

'No, that's why I'm asking you.'

'Four percent of pilots wanna off themselves.'

'I believe they are cranking in the cockpit.' He is always, always smiling.

'Why else would they fly us through here?'

'Because planes are conductors.'

'Of electricity?'

'Of music.'

'But–'

'They are Faraday cages.'

'They're cages?' I say. The woman across the aisle sits ramrod straight and glares.

'We're fine.'

'In Nowhere, we are all in a cage.'

POETRY

That From Afar Looks Like A Poem

Grace Hiu-Yan Wong

Fantastic opening words! that delight and impress
yet as the line progresses, drags on for a bit too long
so that its readers more or less lose interest before its

eventual, overdue, much longed-for full stop. Artistic
attempt to engage readers again. Witty line that is also
mildly provocative. Some readers will not be amused.

Line containing an obnubilated word that either induces
a twenty-three second search in the *OED* for diligent readers,
or is ignored by ones that *have not reached their fullest potential,*

or have trouble concentrating. Brisk line that, for some,
may allude to and reflect current political situations,
followed by semi-apologetic acknowledgement that this

has been done before. Quick revelatory moment
in which the significance of the title becomes apparent.

Happenstance
After Paula Rego

Grace Hiu-Yan Wong

Imagine the landlady's surprise in finding you
at the head of her dining table, sitting so prettily there
in your immaculate dress. With dovelike docility
you perch and labour over her husband's
bog-trodden work boots on her best starched table cloth,
while wearing the shoes that *she* gave away last winter.

The moment when the sun dips in its trajectory
to set your skin aglow, the landlady, recognising
when certain things are rendered irretrievable,
lets the door click back into place. Soft scratches
on the other side splinter into sound –
the cat is clawing to get out again.

Family Affairs

Grace Hiu-Yan Wong

The sixties were unkind.
She learned from a young age
the art of waiting, listening for
the familiar clatter of keys,
her mother's sooty return
from a day of coal-hauling.

Once they turned off all the lights
to lay flat on the floor
when the landlord came
to collect his due, holding
their breath until his footsteps
receded down the hall.

Scraps leftover from meals
were stored in a food cabinet
hanging from the ceiling in chains,
much to the rats' dismay.

After dinners the family would sit
threading plastic flowers,
piercing stems through petals
for a dollar a basket.

Things are better now, she says,
hands working tirelessly still,
scoring each tangerine with a knife before
opening them up into veinous blossoms.

The boy is not convinced. He doesn't like
sharing. While staring at the quartered
segments on the dinner table, he thinks about
the thickened fingers, callused palms –
almost forgives her for marrying his father.

magic beans

Laquerriere

on my desk sits a small pile of packaged pills
in a generic white pharmacy box rationed out
in a batch they said with a reassuring grimace
would not be enough to cause death sometimes
I take the little plastic pods out of the unmarked
box and stack them into pyramids of unjustly
imprisoned yellowy-green jumping beans but
they're otherwise untouched I don't know if
being bestowed with these jaunty capsules
is a step forward or a step back getting help
sounds positive but needing it's the opposite
the graver lows will go at the expense of highs
a flatlined life of mediocrity and detachment
I worry that in losing my extremes I'll lose myself
but then I think I've already lost myself and
that's probably what got me here and whatever's
gone to chemically-induced indifference would
be just as gone if I stepped up onto the decorative
stony edges of North Bridge and walked off
they carry a warning as all such tablets do
that side-effects include suicidal thoughts
the greatest of all ironies, and perhaps what
Hamlet meant when he said '*#YOLO be a
martyr or don't mate you're buggered either
way but life ain't a melodrama*'(3.1.56-60) then
I think I've done crazier things in the name of
survival than swallow a set number of morning
milligrams there's only so many times you can
try to slice a carrot with a spoon or cure injuries
with herbal remedies and wear elasticated clothes
before you realise that removing painkillers
belts and sharp objects from your life is not
a viable long-term plan I think it's time I took
a risk and swapped this heavy half-dead
cow I've been dragging for a chance to see
what's waiting at the other end of all the long
trembling greeny-yellow beanstalk's lianas

REASONS TO LIVE

Laquerriere

car rides to bridlington - sausage sandwiches - hobbits doing
a poor job of feigning heterosexuality - posh unchewed pens -
attractive people who make really good tea - 97% of all cats -
transformations - cheap inoffensive soft furnishings - walking
through windsor with a large upside-down lampshade on your
head - bunting made of knickers strung across a vicarage - naff
home movies - old people calling you 'pet' - unexpected post
from people you give a shit about - crappy christmas films with
violently untalented extras - sarcasm - huge displays of towel
bales in smug department stores – sequinned octogenarians at
the theatre - shit musicals - sharing a stale loaf with demented
ducks - bailey's - novels that necessitate no analysis - coming
home to see your mum's stuck the drawings you sent on the
fridge even though you're 23 and every visitor asks which of the
grandchildren she doesn't have did it - facile sitcoms - retro phone
booths nobody's done a piss in - matching dinnerware - quietly
singing along to hymns with the rude version - hitting jelly with
a cricket bat – whoever writes the overly detailed chocolate
descriptions - fancy old clocks - brunch at the mad hatter's tea
rooms - lending knitwear to someone you like so much you
don't care if they give it back - jazz hands - louis theroux and his
gawking great beak - hot water bottles - three hour plane rides
that weren't preceded by security grabbing your crotch - above
average quality mattresses - novelty soaps - flooding chemistry
classrooms and getting off scot free - horoscopes - making a bell
end of yourself with someone who merrily makes a bell end of
themselves too – eating food off a classroom desk – meaningless
tattoos - professors who conclude their correspondences with
smiley faces :) – bearded drag queens – amateur orchestras
with so many out of tune instruments that they form their own
hilarious but haunting harmonies – bonfire nights hosted by
chubby christians – neighbours who don't make you rethink
your stance on nuclear weapons – unexpected hankies – finding
someone else under the age of forty who uses fabric softener –
mangled sponges salvaged into trifle bases – tolerable haircuts
– building pyramids of bulk bought loo roll and diving into them
– successfully making off unseen with the trolley of leftover free
wine from terribly tedious academic mixers

The Garden

Celia Wilding

I

Wisps of brown hair
float above tangled
rhubarb leaves. She pushes
her hands through, pinching
the ripening pods
of sugar snap peas.

In the shade
(her dress sown from poppies),
she catches oak tree seeds
as they spiral towards the ground.

The chair swing sings back
and forth with the bird calls,
shifting light from the canopy
marking the cushions
like frogspawn.

Windswept bluebell bonnets
litter the patio, the slabs
turning cold
under her bare feet.

II

Bubbles surge
angry hot spittle

                                        the kettle clicks

I pour
scalding water
over yellow paving

                                        black melon pips
                                        take flight from
                                        water-clogged gullies

        'I couldn't live without a garden'

you say as

                        winged ants climb the pebbledash

            'It's my magic place'

my sandals tap against the stone steps

                                        click.

III

Pale hydrangeas
circle the fish pond and moss
covers the rocks once
varnished sparkling blue.

Climbing ivy interferes
with next doors fence,
blackbirds land on dead
hanging baskets and peck
stale soil.

Deluxe

Nathan Watson

i am in great condition.
fat pink flowers, deluxe.
artificial sunsets crackle
in a bowl, an offering
of kinship. browsing the
mist for algorithms, ink
blots pixels & an
illustration of breasts in
Sauna, pornographic blue
(the kind i can never
outstrip) i am under
hot surveillance, synthetic
& stretched across the
Sauna's interface
exporting pink flowers
on the deep deluxe web
close tab>start weeping.
my inbox ejaculates
red rejections, ambient
drone music –
such exquisite content
from the Sauna today.
i am in great condition.
fat, pink, deluxe.
marbled with failures
& shit & susceptible
to paradise.

AV

Nathan Watson

Adjusting TV aerials in
a warm motel over Lake Erie.

Two skeletons in yellow mackintoshes
wave from the forest
like snow-scorpions tapping on glass.

I am looking for distortions,
technicolour static to make the mute
canvas speak.

Later I am drinking gin listening
to a sparrow's falsetto
decompose on subtitles.

Pain has no edge.
Proves inexhaustible.
Can be rearranged.

I unlock my briefcase,
turn on the portable radio,

the television, all the
lights in the motel.

Skeletons crack their polished clavichords
under the night's new bulbs.

We share a Molotov cocktail in the corridor.
It is so bright for once.

I invite them in and show them the negatives.
They keep unspooling
your cassette-tape of sunshine

and playing it backwards to
see how it works – to see
how it looks each time

1600 pennsylvania avenue

Ashley Hugot

as i witnessed your projectile-vomiting hollow promises
to the world all i wanted was to write a poem about
you. i thought that by gathering your mumblings
together in my arms i could paste them onto a clean
canvas and unsay the said. i thought that by catching
your words as you spat them out i could nurse them
– plant fresh seeds inside the pockets of your letters;
allow them to develop anew. but your words gave
me almond hues with droplets of cornsilk, cosmic
latte – hex #F5F5DC. you see, i always thought that
a true artist could compose no matter the material
but like the bile-toned product you supplied me with
my words came out bland. but this colorful planet we
step on today strives on the light so go on and plant
your seeds, we told you. for you always failed to
fertilize, we remained confident nothing could grow.
but today from your flaky foundation sprouted your
frankenstein flowers. i suppose we really should not
have underestimated the nutritive powers of gullibility.
if your ruling extended beyond my metaphor it would
exist as a white snakeroot. skipping the scientific details
– you do not even have to come into direct contact with
white snakeroot to shrivel and die. abraham lincoln's
mother died from white snakeroot infused milk and
it's like now all i see are sick cows potentially tainted
by your toxins just waiting to pass it on to me. except
this mooing primarily echoes from internet links and
passive aggressive tweets. how does it feel to have
your portrait hanging in the internet phenomenon
hall of fame alongside trollface and tommy wiseau
with the harlem shake playing on a loop? you know
we weren't all on our toes waiting for a winner – we
were waiting for you to unzip your flappy deep carrot

orange hex #E9692C flesh and reveal your true color of alien armpit hex #94DE02. we all pretty much just stood there awkwardly thinking gee, ashton kutcher sure is running late. i'll admit throughout the day i still grasped a small morsel of hope that it is all a joke, or a dream – but there's nothing as sobering as having a kkk twitter account harass one of your posts and mock you: the fragile liberal. your success is a defeat for me like i've been beat down by cannons. people are celebrating and my ability to see color has disappeared. confetti looks like old cartoon rain. rose-colored glasses are now a red cap. you know how in the 2004 spongebob squarepants movie plankton creates the CHUM BUCKET BUCKET HELMET that at first seems like a fun accessory for his customers but actually controls their minds allowing him to take over bikini bottom? well we can now all get a new and improved model for the reasonable price of $25 at donaldjtrump. com! and whilst insignificant plankton can fit into the palm of your hand – we know you are perfectly sized and possess long and beautiful fingers amongst other things. we're going to need a bigger sponge to soak up this mess. and while we wait for a sanitary product strong enough to clean up your atomic tangerine hex #FF9966 spillage to be invented we've been told – not to worry! the sun will rise in the morning. funny because no matter the time displayed on my wrist i'm still running nowhere fast on a hamster wheel stuck in some sort of black dawn or a time warp. but maybe i'm overreacting. after all, you did state in your inspirational book entitled CRIPPLED AMERICA (published by threshold editions) that really you're a nice guy. you pride yourself on being a nice guy. i suppose i'm just one in the unstoppable tide of easily offended millennials. time to run to twitter to whine – oh shit never mind there goes that kkk account again. but you know, at the end of the day we may complain but we're not the ones throwing temper tantrums as our bathroom companions refuse to present their genitals to us – like enraged infants baby, boom. my little brother is seven years old and one day he told us he wanted to be president. why? so he could, i quote "say anything he wants". wacky tv personality bill cosby was right about at least one thing – kids do say the darndest things! so stack your blocks of bittersweet shimmer hex #BF4F51 and burnt umber hex #8A3324 and we will master the art of rock-climbing. staple my sin holes – deny me the right to determine whether or not i should procreate and i will create a generation of characters conditioned to fight you. with green dollar bill hex #85BB65 thumbs we will seed this land – witches butter will grow on these dead trees while your army of corpse flowers will disintegrate once and for all. that's it, i'm done with this hysterical babbling – but one last thing: the georgia o'keefe flowers will not be for grabbing.

PRIZE WINNERS

SLOAN PRIZE
WINNER 2017

The Sloan Prize is awarded annually for a prose or verse composition in Lowland Scots vernacular to a matriculated student or to a graduate of the University of Edinburgh of less than three years' standing.

DUNCAN SNEDDON

Duncan Sneddon was born in Edinburgh, and grew up in Pakistan. He is a PhD student at the University of Edinburgh, working on early medieval Scotland, but also works on Gaelic literature. He has published several short stories and non-fiction pieces in Scots, and also produces Scots translations of prose and poetry from several other languages.

ATWEEN THE STORMS

Auld Tam hotched his shooders and pulled his duddie hap tichter aroond him agin the cauld. He leukit up at the whitely sun, whae sailed indifferently i the lift, her mind on her ain affairs, an wi nae time tae spare tae warm Tam's chilled banes. The waves rowed sleepily tae the straund, the sea haein spent aw its fury the nicht afore. *An whit a fury.* The sea haed dung the shore like sae monie smiths haimmerin at an anvil, an the dementit skraich o the wund whippin in aff the watter haedna lat up aw nicht. *Aye, an the bluidy dreep-dreep through the roof, an aw. Oh! Ma bluidy knee!* He stappit for a bittie, steikit his een, an lat the dull throb fade frae his richt knee. It'd be back again afore lang – ayeweys wis i the cauld

164

wedder.

Young Tam – his dochter's lad – haed gaed on aheid o him, leukin for onie widd that micht hae been kest up on the straund. There'd been naething sae faur the day but blibbans o seaweed, but ye nivver kent a storm micht bring. *Whaur's he gotten tae?* The lad haed roonditt the corner o the clift, an wis noo oot o sicht. A guid lad, an though he wis jist shy o seiven years, wis awready taw getting. Strang, an aw. *It'll no be lang afore he's oot i the boat himsel. Jist as weill, for I'll no be able tae dae it an affie lot langer masel. Oh, this bluidy knee!*

Syne o a suddentie, Young Tam cam skelpin back aroond the clift-bend, ower the weit saund, rinnin tae Auld Tam as fast as his legs wad tak him.

'GrampaTam! GrampaTam!'

'Aye lad! Aye lad! Whit's aw this, are ye aw richt?'

'Grampa... Tam!' the lad arrived, pechin haird and fechtin for air. 'There's a... deid horse on the straund!'

'A deid horse?'

'Aye, it maun hae taen a faw doon... the clift, puir beast! It's a muckle yin. Jist up... roond the...' mair pechin, 'roond the clift-bend, there.' He streitched oot his airm, an pyntit. 'Aye, a deid horse. A broon yin!'

'Weill, lat's gae for a deek, than.'

'An a man, an aw.'

'A whit!'

'A man. There's a man jist there richt nixt the horse, he's deid an aw.'

Auld Tam could feel a cauld wecht in his stamack, an he hirpled quickly alang the straund, his knee screamin aw the while, Young Tam rinnin on aheid. An there they were, richt eneuch. A lairge, broon horse, an, jist a few yairds awa, a man. Auld Tam didna need a lang leuk tae see they were baith stane deid. The man's hause-bane wis twistit obscenely, an his richt airm bent awa aw unnaitural-like. There wis nae licht in the een that stared oot across the slate-grey watters, an a blueness haed came ower his skin. No a young man, but no yit auld, wi streaks o grey in his daurk hair an short, weill-clippit baird. His claes leukit gey fine – his hap wis lined wi fur an fastened wi a gowden chain, his ridin buits were o guid, stoot ledder. Gowden rings on his fingers. A bonnie dirk in a richly-decorate ledder scabard wis on his belt. *A nobleman, than. But I dinna ken his face.* Auld Tam thocht for a mament aboot helpin himsel tae the rings, an onie siller he micht find i the man's pooches. *But they'll be missed. Fowk'll be comin leukin for this man, aye. Whae is he? Weill, he'll no be ridin awa frae here, that's for shair, aye.*

He turned to leuk at the horse, an saw Young Tam hunkert doon by it, tryin tae lowse the saidle. *Och, an he'd no be daein on this beast, either.* Baith o its front legs had snappit, there wis a reid bluidy faem at its mooth, an the saund aw aboot whaur it liggit wis churned up. *Puir craiture.* She maun hae thrashed aboot in a panic whan she cam doon the clift, brakkin her legs an throwin her maister. *I howp his end wis quicker.*

'Leave the saidle an the gear alane, Young Tam, it's no oors.'

'Whit happened, Grampa? An dae ye ken whae he is?'

'It maun hae been as ye said, Young Tam. The man'll hae been ridin alang the sea-gate last nicht, an the horse'll hae fawn doon the clift i the storm. I dinna ken whae the man is, but he maun be hie-born, frae his claes an gear. Hie-born, but wantin gumption, takkin the sea-gate at nicht in a storm like thon. Whitever gart him dae sic a glaikit thing, I wunner? Weill, he's peyed for it.'

'Whit shid we dae? Shid we burry thaim? I'll rin hame an get the spade. An Faither William.' Auld Tam smiled. 'Weill, he'll –'

'*They'll.*'

'*They'll* need a proper Christian yirdin, o coorse. But, we canna yird him here on this straund. This is a hie-born man, an he'll hae his ain lair nae doot. An his friends'll come leukin for him tae tak him awa tae it. They'll want tae ken whit happened. Whae kens? They micht gie ye a wee sumthing tae thank ye for findin him.'

Auld Tam wis prood tae see Young Tam tried tae hide hoo pleased the thocht made him.

'The puir horse,' said Young Tam. 'I ken a man's mair imporant, Grampa, but she's sic a bonnie mare. I've no seen the like.'

'Aye.' There didna seem a lot else tae say, sae he didna say ocht. Efter a meinute, he crossed himsel, an gestured tae Young Tam tae dae likwise. Mair silence, brakken ainlie by the lappin o the watter an the faur-aff skraich o a gull.

Auld Tam gaed back tae the man, shut his een, an wi Young Tam's help set him oot straucht, wi his haunds fauldit on his breist. *A mair dignifee'd wey for his friends tae see him.* 'Weill,' he said, 'we canna dae onie mair for him here.' Mair silence. Young Tam crossed himsel again.

Noo. Tae get this man awa frae here. The best thing wad be tae get tae the toon, an pass on the news there. That wis ower faur for Young Tam tae gae his lane, sae he wis left ahint tae leuk efter the bodie. *An tae mak siccar that nae birds or ither siclike things come tae fash it.* Auld Tam wad heid for the toon himsel. The brae wis ower stey for his knee, sae tae get up ontae the sea-gate, he'd need tae gae the lang wey roond – anither hauf-mile tae whaur the wee burn ran intae the sea. Whan he got tae the burn, he hunkert doon (*painfully*), cupped his haunds, an teuk a lang draucht o cauld watter. The day wisna hot, an the sun abuin aye haed mair on her mind nor sendin warmth doon tae Fife, but Auld Tam haed felt his mooth affy dry. Forbye, he'd no planned on a lang walk whan he set oot this mornin, an didna hae a skin o watter wi him. *Or ocht stranger, mair's the peity*.

As he stuid up, aince mair pullin his hap ticht aroond him, he saw faur aff twa horsemen ridin north alang the sea-gate, gaein fast, but haudin ticht by the clift-edge. *They micht be leukin for him*. Auld Tam decidit tae staund by the gate, an hail thaim whan they cam near. Afore lang, they drew close by, an he could see frae their rich claes an the swuirds on their belts that they were indeed noblemen. He raised his richt airm an cawed oot, 'Haw, Sirs!' They pulled up, an walked their horses alang tae him, but didna dismoont. They were reid-faced, pechin, an haed clearly been ridin haird for sum time.

167

Yin o thaim, whae maun hae jaloused Auld Tam tae be a begger, teuk a smaw coin frae his purse an tossed it tae him. 'Guid day, auld yin. Whit for did ye cry us ower? We hae nae time tae spare ye, an maun on oor wey.'

'I dinna seek yer coin, Sir, though I thank ye for it. I hae news.'

'News?'

'Aye, Sirs. Dae ye seek a nobleman, sic as yersels?'

'That we dae. Hae ye seen yin?'

'Aye, Sirs. A weill-dressed, bairdit man wi a broon horse an a dirk – ma lad fund him on the straund no an hour syne.'

'Fund him?' said the saicont yin, 'Tell us, man, is he weill? We hae missed sic a man syne lest nicht, an monie men are seekin him.'

'Alas,' said Auld Tam, 'he is deid. Yer friend maun hae taen a faw doon the clift i the storm. He wis lang deid whan I saw him, Sirs.'

The colour drained frae their faces, leavin thaim baith pale an seik-leukin. 'Deid?' said the first man. 'Ye are siccar o't?'

'I am. I am sairry tae say it, Sirs. I can tak ye tae him, it isna faur frae here.' The saicont man slumped in his saidle, as gin the life were leavin him an aw. '*O Columba, spes Scotorum,*' he muttert.

'Lord abuin help us,' said the first, kestin his een up tae the lift, whaur the sun aye rowed on, aye peyin nae mind. 'The keing is deid. The keing is deid.'

❈

Qwhen Alexander our kynge was dede,

That Scotlande lede in lauche and le,

Away was sons of alle and brede,

Off wyne and wax, of gamyn and gle.

Our golde was changit in to lede.

Christ, borne in virgynyte,

Succoure Scotlande, and ramade,
That stade is in perplexitie.[1]

---

1 Anon, c. 1300. Text taen frae Thomas Owen Clancy (ed.), *The Triumph Tree: Scotland's Earliest Poetry, AD 550 – 1350* (Edinburgh: Canongate, 1998), p. 297.

HAIKU FOR REFUSED HEARTS

#5
I'm awkward for you.
I'm a hunched weeping willow
With untied laces.

#29
Text message alert,
Running from a cold shower,
It wasn't from him.

#35
I slept with someone
Else to teach you a lesson.
You were out of town.

#41
I call the cat in.
His name leans back in my mouth;
Real as a tattoo.

#44
Lipstick on a glass,
Wooly hat under the bed.
Will you just leave, please?

#49
I see her rushing,
Kicking up leaves in her wake.
I keep on rushing.

#50
Christmas Eve party,
Across the room he's laughing.
Helplessness rages.

#67
I hope I'll see her
Crossing a snow laden street
Until I see her.

#82
I think about him
Less and less but never less
Than every winter.

LEWIS EDWARDS PRIZE WINNER 2017

This prize was established in memory of Lewis Edwards, who died while a student of English Literature at the University. It is open to any matriculated undergraduate student of the University of Edinburgh.

PAULA COLMENARES LEÓN

Paula comes from Spain, one of those South European countries that, according to the Eurogroup president, waste their money on drinks and women. As 'countries' nowadays still come to implicitly stand for 'men', and women are placed in the same category as alcohol, Paula is trying to find a voice (and a place!). She can't locate herself yet, but since the study places usually take that function in a short bio of someone who is still studying, it could be mentioned that she studies at the Universidad Complutense de Madrid, as well as in the Escuela Contemporánea de Humanidades, and is now on an Erasmus scholarship at the University of Edinburgh. She normally writes in Spanish because her experience is in that language. She would like you to reach her on paulacolmenares@gmail.com so that she could stop referring to herself in the third person!

FAMILY SECRETS: A CASE STUDY

'So, if you were to highlight anything in that paragraph, would you use the red or the blue highlighter? Remember the code,' said Julia. Juan and Julia used to borrow books from the library of Julia's father, who was a doctor and an antiquarian book dealer. They decided that adults had secrets, and books had secrets because they were written in the language of adults, so they would create a secret language to unravel the secrets of the adult language. And if her father or any other adult read the book, they would not even notice there was a secret language and unwritten things going on there, they would instead think: 'just kids' stuff.'

Julia and Juan developed the following, as an adult would say, complex and clever method of highlighters: how thick the felt tip, how fluorescent the ink, what colour, how straight the drawn line, whether it was underlying or covering the words; 5 features that were graded each according to 5 distinguishable parameters, that made 125 possible combinations. Each combination was a syllable, which was a bit precarious, but for kids challenges are sweet like popping candy, until they grow up. They would write what they had understood from their reading using that method.

Then Julia began to feel slightly uneasy. If Julia had mastered the adult language by then, she would have expressed that, for her, the point of a secret language was that it could be spotted as a secret language. It had to be obscure, but not as much so as to miss that there was a language being spoken there. It had to incite a feeling that you were being excluded from something that continued its course of life without you. That was what a secret entailed, she would have argued. Julia expressed her uneasiness in different terms, which made her uneasiness a completely different one.

On another unfortunate occasion, when Juan became tired of all the combinations, he said: 'But a secret should not be something that is so difficult to create, I mean, what is difficult is not to create them, right?' Julia did not want to give up on their pursuit so they argued bitterly.

Then circumstances changed: their high schools were in different counties. But they did not keep track of the process of their separation, as they grew up without noticing, and forgot both the language and the argument. There was no bittersweet memory, no troubled thought, no sense of loss.

Julia did not see the teenagers at high school as people with whom she shared a secret. Teenagers had not been trained in hiding their flaws, they revealed what they tried to conceal, and concealed what was worthy of praise.

Adults were different. When she was ten her father was going to leave home and move to a nearby city and he said: 'Nothing is going to change. I'm going to pick you up and take you to school every morning.' Julia said: 'But why,' and her mother looked at her father, and her father said: 'We will tell you once you are sixteen.'

'Can I tell Juan and Sara tomorrow in school?' said Julia, once the conversation was over.

'Well, it's not that you can't, it's that it may be something you want to keep to yourself, something private.'

Julia felt embarrassed. Had she not noticed it was something private? She nodded. She told neither Juan nor Sara.

The day after, her father did not leave home, nor the day after that, nor the day after that. Julia did not ask.

Her parents talked more or less in the usual way. Gradually they started sharing more inside jokes and laughing at them, fewer silences started to happen. After a while she was convinced her father was not going to leave.

'Secrecy has been identified as detrimental for mutual trust and understanding and is negatively related to the quality of the personal relationship,' Julia read somewhere. Bruno's train of thought presumably led him to a very different conclusion, and he would even say: 'Lying is proof of intelligence in young children,' and would smile proudly as if that could apply to himself, even though he was no longer a young child.

The first time Bruno and Julia met, Bruno had said his mother was ill so she had moved to Andalucía to treat her illness. 'What does she have,' asked Julia, and Bruno said, 'It's a rare disease.' 'But which one?' asked Julia, and Bruno said, 'A rare disease, I cannot remember the name, it was rare as well.' Julia wondered whether that was a joke, but Bruno said gravely: 'You know, very few people know this, I never talk about it.' When they said goodbye and went back to their houses, Julia felt she was being pushed to a level of intimacy she did not want to reach so quickly, and felt reluctant to meet him again. In the following months,

Bruno did not mention anything about his mother, though.

Julia asked once, and Bruno said he did not feel like talking about it. They would spend a lot of time watching TV in Bruno's house. Sometimes Bruno remained silent for hours. Julia imagined his mind, in those time-leaps, black and guttural like the mouth of a wolf. When Julia asked, he said, 'It's complicated,' and remained black and guttural.

Bruno once said to her: 'You don't have hobbies.' Julia said, 'I do, I like reading.' Bruno said: 'That's not a hobby. Hobbies are playing basketball, or chess, or watching films, or politics.' Those were his hobbies. 'You just gossip, that's all you and your girlfriends do when you get together.' Julia did not have many girlfriends, and distance grew steadily between them as she and Bruno grew closer.

Julia had met Bruno in the last year of high school, and they moved to a flatshare for the first year of university. There was another thing Bruno had assumed Julia did not have: secrets. Why did Bruno want, then, to have her? Julia did not know what the answer for Bruno was.

When Bruno kissed her, Julia tried to see the moist ball that was his tongue as she felt it, but looking downwards, found nothing. He did know how to kiss, but she couldn't explain what the kissing process was.

Bowel movements are the end result of the body taking the nutrients it needs from the food one eats and execrating waste from the body, and normally people don't want to let others have an insight into their digestive process. In a flatshare you can't help but being acquainted with the frequency, colour, smell and sometimes even shape and size, of the waste of the others. Everyone keeps their insights to themselves.

Bruno left a greenish trail in the toilet and its texture was like that of the paint that kids use when finger painting. The food typically takes three days from the time it is eaten until it finishes its journey in the toilet, and if it takes a shorter time, the result may be greener stool because green is one of the first colours in the rainbow of the digestive process. In such terms Julia's father told things to Julia when she was younger. Bruno's greener stool made sense, for 'Bruno processes radical change rather fast. Too fast, you know, sometimes he even seeks it,' said Julia to Claire in the kitchen, and so the product was that greenish finger-paint stool.

Claire, the other flatmate in the flatshare, used to run the sink to cover the noise of her bowel movements. Julia was impressed by how successful she was, how she could do things without letting others noticing.

There were two bathrooms in the flat. The walls were adjoined. Sometimes two people would poop in the adjacent rooms and both could tell, because of the heavy silence that precedes and follows such events in the bathroom, as if they were sacred. Claire and Bruno shared the sacredness and the silences more often than Julia and Bruno did, they went to the bathroom and came back to their rooms at the same time, coordinately.

After the conversation with her parents that day, Julia overheard something that she was not meant to hear, when her mother was talking with a friend of hers. What she heard she could not remember properly, but it had to do with: 'he,' 'two weeks in France,' 'but instead here with her.'

Julia could not sleep that well for a couple of days, she could hear her mother typing on her computer, and her father typing on his too. Her mother in the study, her father in the library.

When Julia could not sleep, she imagined herself stepping out of bed and running into her mother's arms and soothing her mother's sorrow by telling her she knew; that image was followed by how she would then have to run to her father's arms and tell him nothing was going to change. But if they had decided not to tell her until she was sixteen, it was because her father thought she would stop loving him if she knew. Convinced that she was too immature to not stop loving, he would become very angry with her mother for having broken their agreement. In addition, Julia could not run that fast from one parent to the other, and the two events would overlap.

Julia read sociological papers on family secrets and had to read much more before taking action, until she was fully sure of the implications of revealing her secret. In the meantime, she waited, until she forgot her initial goal of taking action and experienced time as time and not as meantime.

Sometimes, especially when her birthday came, Julia became anxious imagining how the conversation would take place; wondering if on the day of her sixteenth birthday she was going to go downstairs and find the faces of her parents hovering above the sofa, waiting for her, obscured like two thick drops of blood, the sofa hard and sectional like an operating table.

On that sofa she would tell them the truth, maybe even before his father told it all. She would say: 'I have known it since I was ten.' And they would tell her, 'All this time — and you knew?' They would marvel at her maturity.

Some of the jokes between her parents were in fact her mother's reproaches, that they thought only the two of them understood. Such jokes eased her mother's sorrow.

Julia kept her secret, as well as her parents kept theirs. She caressed it, and it grew as a loving, respectful, God-fearing, healthy girl; was soft as tissue paper, and heavy as a toilet tank.

'Keeping a secret is the first step in becoming an individual. Telling is the second step,' read a quote by a so-called Tournier at the beginning of an essay on family secrets. When Julia was in high school and read this, she was a bit proud to have become an individual, if she were to be honest, but did not know when to take the second step, so she continued reading essays. She also looked up reliable information on how to kiss, when she was in high school: she just could not imagine how that could be pleasurable, faultless and rhythmical.

When Bruno and Julia were still in high school, they used to spend hours talking on the phone. Julia had not planned to tell Bruno her family secret, and certainly would not have done it that way if planned, but Bruno used the condescending tone of someone who does have hobbies to suggest she could not imagine the distressing family panorama he had in childhood, because her family was perfect. It would take a couple of years more for Julia to think that masculinity was deciding what a hobby is and what is not, and what can affect a child and what cannot. Probably, also what a child can know and what a child cannot know, but Julia would not dare to say such things, she had to read more essays. Julia told Bruno on the phone, briefly, what she remembered from her father's adultery, taking the second step in becoming an individual. It took less than a month for Bruno to forget it, for he was busy remembering his mother had first left his father for a new lover, and ultimately also left Bruno, departing with that new lover and her heroin addiction to Andalucía. Bruno never clearly stated his mother was addicted to heroin, nor pinpointed the fact that she left with a new lover so, for years, it was still difficult for Julia to tell which of the two was the rare disease, the heroin addiction or the lover.

In the flat, sometimes Julia would reproach Bruno, as if she were joking, and Claire used to laugh at this. At first, Julia thought maybe Claire could find such a situation uncomfortable, suddenly exposed to the intimacies of their relationship, but Claire used to say: 'I could listen to both of you for hours,' and then she threw up rough, partially digested yellowish laughs; her abdominal muscles, inspiratory muscles and the diaphragm going through a series of coordinated contractions and then releasing pressure and expulsing the vomitus of such private, loud laughter.

One day, Julia and Bruno finally had an argument in the kitchen, when Claire was around. At the end, Claire approached Bruno, her slippers sticking to the dirty kitchen floor like an animal with suction pads, and kissed him in the forehead, a brief kiss that sounded like a slug being squashed. Then, Claire kissed Julia briefly too, and said they'd better forget about it. Julia wondered if it was she who was being exposed to the intimacy of another relationship.

In the first year of high school, Julia took advantage of an anecdote somewhat connected with her parents' aborted divorce. The issue could lurk for years and only emerge intensely for a couple of months before vanishing. That anecdote happened when the issue was floating in her mind like used toilet paper on the toilet bowl so, while in the car, she asked her father: 'Why did you not leave in the end?'

Her father smiled as if lost in remembrance and said: 'Because you were so worried about my feeling lonely, constantly saying I should live in that new place with some friend. I couldn't leave you with such worries.' That was the last thing Julia would have expected.

It's important to note that her father constantly made jokes, whether he was being asked something of importance or not. When one was expecting him to then separate the truth from the joke, answering a sentence clear like a surgical incision, he would not add anything.

To Julia, masculinity was also being able to remain silent when an explanation would normally be requested. The explanation arrived so late that it brought embarrassment with it. In the last year of high school, she heard a constant rumour, like a toilet flushing, that went: 'Is Julia stupid?' Or: 'Why is Julia still with Bruno?' For Julia, the question was why Bruno was still with her, or, if he was stupid.

When Julia turned fourteen she thought maybe her parents were already prepared and wished, secretly, they weren't.

When Julia turned sixteen she knew it was not going to happen. She felt embarrassed about having thought they were going to have such a formal meeting. How little did she control the language of adults: how little did she know that sometimes what was said was not meant, but was intended to bring transitory comfort — 'We'll tell you once you are sixteen' — and that non-spoken words were more important than what was said, because non-spoken words were meant, and they were to bring lasting sorrow.

'With you I don't feel lonely,' said Bruno. But with Julia he did feel lonely, and maybe it was only with both Julia, and with another woman that was not called Julia, at that very precise moment, Claire, that he did not feel lonely.

If Bruno did not want to find out when and why Julia remained silent, Julia had spent so much time trying to find out what his silences covered, and she had not been able to weigh which sentences, out of the ones Bruno said aloud, were more important. The 'With you I don't feel lonely' one seemed to explain a whole relationship. It was something Bruno had said several times. He did not consider it a secret, so Julia had not considered it a secret, either. Only when being given a summarising quality, did it become a heavy truth.

As she gave Claire her keys, she thought the problem with secrets was that people were inept enough to let outsiders know they kept a secret, but not the content of it. And with shared-secrets people were incompetent enough to let outsiders know they had kept a secret, but not the crucial points about it. All she had wanted since childhood was something that kept happening to her without her knowing it, something that continued its course of life under her absolute unawareness. Julia and her secrets happened to Bruno under Bruno's absolute unawareness.

Julia left the flatshare and went back to her parents for a short period, until she could find another. Once at home, she went to her father's library and browsed some books. Two of them had the marks of her childhood endeavours with Juan. Her father came in when she was taking a look at one and said, bemused: 'When did you do this to my books, and why? I must say, first time I found it, it did not amuse me.' Julia said: 'Kids' stuff.' She remembered they meant something, but did not know what. She probably thought, in the exclamatory mode, how she had lost her childhood without noticing. In response to her father's insistent queries, Julia said: 'It looks like a complex and clever method of highlighters. I can't remember the code.' Her father said, 'It's a shame, we will never know young Julia's secrets.'

CONTRIBUTORS

- CONTRIBUTORS -

JOSEPHINE A. was a journalism graduate before becoming a creative writing postgraduate student. She is originally from Greece and believes that it's better if you don't know her Greek name, as even Greeks can't pronounce it correctly. Her greatest influences are a couple of good books she had the fortune to read before she got addicted to the internet and her ardent curiosity about the human species. In addition to her writing endeavors, she had a short career as an internet radio broadcaster. She likes singing and playing the ukulele and she is decent and mediocre at them respectively.

CONTACT: s1681042@ed.ac.uk, @JosephineAthans

ZACK ABRAMS is originally from North Carolina. He graduated from UNC-Chapel Hill and was in AmeriCorps prior to attending The University of Edinburgh for his MSc in Creative Writing. His fiction has appeared in *Cellar Door* and *Raleigh Magazine*. Dr. Tom Phillips is his strongest influence.

CONTACT: zwabrams@gmail.com

VICTORIA ROSE BALL is an illustrator based in Edinburgh. Her work focuses on illustration, architecture and typography - often combining these to create detailed and quirky pieces in her own unique style.

CONTACT: victoriaroseball.com

RACHANA BHATTACHARJEE is currently a student of the MSc Creative Writing course at The University of Edinburgh. Before that, she worked with various literary start-ups and an NGO in New Delhi, while doing a Bachelor's degree in English Literature. So far, she has sparsely published stories and non-fiction in local magazines and newspapers in India. She writes, drawing on the variety of experiences she has gathered from her life in the many different parts of that country, wanting to inspire people to tell their stories freely through the written word. The lives that she has known, by whatever means, have been the greatest influences on her work.

CONTACT: s1614646@sms.ed.ac.uk, tiyabudi@gmail.com
Twitter: @Rachana420

- CONTRIBUTORS -

CASSIDY COLWELL is a fiction writer originally from Los Angeles, California. Her work has appeared in *Mosaic*. She graduated cum laude from the University of California, Riverside with a Bachelor's degree in Creative Writing. She has worked as a fiction editor for the *Los Angeles Review of Books* and the inaugural issue of *50GS*, a new online literary magazine. She now lives with her boyfriend and their cat in Edinburgh.

CONTACT: cassidycolwell@yahoo.com, *Twitter*: @CossidyCalwell

JACQUELYN CHAPMAN is a writer from Southern California. She loves stories that have elements of magic and writes mostly for young adults and children.

CONTACT: SparkOfaStar@gmail.com

SRISHTI CHAUDHARY is a student of Creative Writing in Edinburgh and studied English Literature before that. Weather usually determines her mood. Her favorite subjects to write about are people, yet she pities the human condition.

RONNIE CHATAH created and led Walk Beirut, a walking tour company that brought Lebanese politics and history to life through storytelling. The tour ran until December 2013, and was forced to end following the assassination of Ronnie's father, Mohamad Chatah, a Lebanese politician devoted to Lebanese sovereignty. Ronnie left Lebanon in 2014, determined to preserve his father's legacy by championing a shared cause – achieving justice through the written word. He is currently working on a short-story collection titled *Tales of a Tour Guide* that reflects on recent Lebanese history, by intertwining his own life in Beirut and his father's final years.

CONTACT: s1580047@ed.ac.uk

PAULA ESPINOSA VALAREZO was born and raised in Quito, Ecuador. She is currently pursuing a Master Degree in Creative Writing in The University of Edinburgh. She is a bilingual short story writer of dreams, and imagination. She considers her writing to be part of the Latin American tradition of Magic Realism and The Fantastic.

She is also a decent cook, a doodler, and loves having friends over at her house.

CONTACT: paula.espinosav@gmail.com

Instagram: @paulaespinosavalarezo

MARK FLANAGAN is, at the time of writing this, a student in the Edinburgh Creative Writing MSc. Originally from Upstate New York, he moved to Scotland to pursue his dream job of staying at home all day and making things up for a living. Outside of some newspaper work, he has yet to be published although he has been rejected by a few prestigious journals. He likes reading things that are sad and funny and thus tries to write within those parameters.

CONTACT: s1678060@ed.ac.uk or markflanagan05@gmail.com

YUTONG FU graduated from Shanghai International Studies Univeristy and got her Bachelor's Degree of Art in June 2016, majoring in English Literature. She is currently studying Msc Creative Writing (fiction) at The University of Edinburgh. During the autumn semester of her junior year, she went to Royal Holloway, University of London as a student of the Study Abroad Program, and took the undergraduate creative writing course and other relevant classes there.

CONTACT: s1616962@ed.ac.uk

MARK HOLMES was born and raised in Newcastle upon Tyne, and started writing stories when he was eight years old. Having previously worked as a barman, a carpenter, and a bookseller, Mark has written a variety of articles on film, football, comedy and music for *NARC Magazine*, *WhatCulture.com*, *The Journal*, and *The Crack*. In his spare time, he enjoys grain alcohol, flourish and whittling. He supports Leeds United.

CONTACT: mhmarkhlms@gmail.com

ASHLEY HUGOT is a poetry student in Edinburgh. She grew up in the United States and France then moved to England at 20. There, she began her academic studies in creative writing and eventually published a collection of poetry and photography entitled *Lady*. Although her poetry is recently politically themed, in the past she would take great interest in writing about the body as she underwent life-changing spinal fusion surgery in 2011. Aside from her artistic interests, she is also one of those people who will go out of her way to pet a dog and probably cry while doing so.

JESSICA IRISH is a writer from Santa Cruz, California. She received her Bachelor's Degree in English at the University of California, Davis, and is currently pursuing her Masters in Creative Writing at The University of Edinburgh. She is an editor for *50GS* and *From Arthur's Seat*. Her influences include works by Margaret Atwood, Cormac McCarthy, Ali Smith, and women who sing about their feelings. She is currently writing a novel about a group of friends struggling to survive during a time of environmental decline, which she hopes will feel fictional for a few more years.

CONTACT: jessica.e.irish@gmail.com; *Twitter*: @frondslikethese

MEGAN JONES was a project manager for a translation company in London before she decided to pursue her dream of being perennially broke and came to study the MSc in Creative Writing at The University of Edinburgh. Her influences include Johnathan Franzen (particularly those long, ranting paragraphs) and John Boyne, because of his mastery of plot, a foreign concept to her. She thinks her writing is funny, a notion confirmed by at least one member of her immediate family.

CONTACT: mc-jones@live.co.uk

LAQUERRIERE is a sort-of poet who writes in a range of styles about everything from Ed Miliband, to mental health issues, to receiving unsolicited photographs of phalluses. They are a graduate of the University of Hull, where they were educated in the art of clowning, the history of madness, and how to turn gender-neutral toilets into performance spaces.

ELENA STURK LUSSIER is from Canada. She spends a lot of time struggling to be witty and she doesn't own a cat. She's published fiction, non-fiction, and poetry in small Canadian journals. Most of her inspiration stems from her dysfunctional family and the Canadian wilderness. Once, she tried to write erotica.

JAMES MACHELL is from London, England. He received his BA in English Literature and Creative Writing from the University of East Anglia, having studied for two semesters at the University of Utrecht. He is also a member of the National Youth Theatre and studying for a Creative Writing MSc at The University of Edinburgh. He predominantly writes science fiction and his influences include Thomas Pynchon, William Gibson, and Neal Stephenson. He has been published in several magazines and is working on his first novel, a space opera set in 2560.

CONTACT: s1671486@sms.ed.ac.uk

MICHAEL S. MARSHALL is a nationality-confused British-Canadian writer; he got his start as award winning cannon fodder at drama festivals in Toronto, as a playwright, and as a dive-bar musician – ergo his employment history reads like a list of state mandated community service jobs.

CONTACT: michaelsmarshall2@gmail.com,
           Twitter: @aDrayofSquirrel

CAITLIN MALONE MCLAUGHLIN is known for her fairly controversial belief in judging books by their covers. This peculiar notion has gotten her the position of designer and typesetter for a number of literary journals, including this one. When she's not debating typefaces on her blog or illustrating her favourite characters, she enjoys crafting the interior aspects of novels and short stories. Her narratives demonstrate her unique perspective on the world. She presents her critical eye, but keeps a rose-colored monocle in her back pocket, infusing magical, often botanical, elements into everyday interactions.

CONTACT: malone.mcl@gmail.com, *Instagram*: @deebsbydesign
           Website: buttonsinthemilkjar.weebly.com

ZOE MCMILLIN is a writer from British Columbia, Canada. She previously studied art history and creative writing at the University of Victoria. She cites her influences as Isabel Allende, Anne Enright, Gabriel García Márquez and Zadie Smith, but her favourite storytellers remain her grandparents. When she isn't taking inspirational walks on the west coast she can be found writing over a cup of tea. She is currently working on a collection of short stories and a novel.

CONTACT: s1679758@ed.ac.uk

VASSILENA PARASHKEVOVA is a Bulgarian who arrived in Britain in 2000, on a coach across Europe and clutching a PhD scholarship. She is co-editor of the *Journal of Commonwealth* Literature (ex-assistant-sleuth/editor at *Clues: A Journal of Detection*) and author of *Salman Rushdie's Cities* (Bloomsbury, 2013). She lives in London with her partner, resisting daily the temptation to fictionalise him, teaching literature, dabbling in the dark arts of interpreting, writing and blending coffee with equal alchemical enthusiasm.

CONTACT: vparashkevova@gmail.com

THEA MARIE RISHOVD is from Norway. She completed her undergraduate MA English Language and Literature at The University of Edinburgh in 2016. She writes mainly literary short fiction. She likes fiction that plays with language and voice. Her main areas of interest are metafiction and the relationship created between the author, the text, and the reader. Her influences include David Foster Wallace, Tom Vowler, Adam Marek and Emily Mackie.

CONTACT: s1142664@sms.ed.ac.uk

JOSH SIMPSON is a student in the MSc in Creative Writing program at The University of Edinburgh. He previously practised law for ten years in Miami, Florida, USA, and now focuses on writing fiction. His short stories have been published in a number of literary journals and he has edited and contributed to @IncitingSparks and is a founding editor of *50GS*, a creative arts journal. He is also an alumnus of the Yale Writers' Conference and was accepted to the Bread Loaf Writers' Conference for 2017. You can find him at joshksimpson@icloud.com and @misterjsim on Twitter.

ELVIS SOKOLI is from New Jersey by way of Albania, although he tells people he's from New York. He studied finance before making the switch to literature and writing, and he definitely does not regret it one bit, believe you me. When he isn't writing, he fancies himself

a Kanye West scholar and whiskey aficionado. He once drank with
Charles MacLean who (drunkenly) told him he has a great nose for
whiskey.

CONTACT: 1elvissokoli@gmail.com

DREW TAYLOR is a Scottish writer born and based in
Edinburgh. He writes humorous and surreal short stories often about
daily life, and has ambitions of writing novels. His favourite authors
include Haruki Murakami, Terry Pratchett, and Cormac McCarthy,
but enjoys reading whatever he can get his hands on. His background
is in film. He previously worked for Scottish Documentary Institute,
and has written several short films as well as the script for an interactive
tourist app based around Edinburgh and its history.

CONTACT: s1680912@ed.ac.uk

DREW TOWNSEND is a graduate of The University of
Aberdeen where he studied English Literature.

CONTACT: andrewtownsend16@hotmail.com

JAMES J. VALLIERE is originally from Midland, Michigan.
He completed his undergraduate at Central Michigan University
where he graduated magna cum laude. Currently, he is perusing a
masters from The University of Edinburgh. His previous work has
been published in *The Central Review*. James describes himself as a
proud Slytherin who is hopelessly in love with Darth Vader and
Superman, a strange dichotomy, he knows…A writer of horror and
the fantastic, his greatest inspirations are Stephen King, Neil Gaiman,
and Thomas Ligotti. Above all else, the love of his life is his best friend,
Lady, objectively the most beautiful and perfect chocolate Labrador.

CONTACT: jamievllr@gmail.com

FRANCESCA VAVOTICI was born and raised in Italy before
moving to the UK at the age of 19. Her passion for literature manifests
itself both in her creative and academic pursuits: she is currently
completing an MSc in Creative Writing, which will be followed by

a PhD in English Literature. She can usually be found drinking hot chocolate in a café or typing away at her vintage typewriter.

CONTACT: f.vavotici@gmail.com, *Instagram/Twitter:* @fravavotici

RAYMOND VERMEULEN is a Dutch writer and narrative designer who is currently living in the UK. He majored in Philosophy of Science at university, a move widely panned by critics. His work on technology and esotericism has been featured prominently on both his fridge and his corkboard. Like his stories, Raymond is both multimedia and interactive. Don't hesitate to get in touch through email or Twitter if you have a project you would like to collaborate on together.

CONTACT: raymond.vermeulen@gmail.com, @raymondvrmln

NATHAN WATSON holds a BA in American Literature with Creative Writing from UEA. He currently lives in Scotland where he is studying an Msc in Creative Writing at The University of Edinburgh and working on his first collection. His work has appeared in a number of magazines including *Lighthouse Literary Journal, The Elbow Room, Butcher's Dog* and *The Cadaverine.* All writing appears under Nathaniel King, and can be found at nathanielking.tumblr.com

GRACE HIU-YAN WONG was born and raised in Hong Kong. She studied English Language and Literature at the Hong Kong Baptist University, where she was a co-founding editor of the creative journal *EDGE.* Her poetry explores places, memories and human relationships. Apart from reading and writing, her interests include photography, nature walks, and learning about the names of plants.

CONTACT: whygracewrites@gmail.com; *Twitter:* @whygracewrites

JESSICA WIDNER has a BA in English Literature from the University of Toronto, and is currently completing an Msc in Creative Writing at the University of Edinburgh. Her work has appeared in *Ceramic Dog Magazine, Potluck Mag*, and *Lantern Magazine.*

CELIA WILDING is a poet and comedian from the Lake District studying MSc Creative Writing at UoE. She holds a BA in Creative Writing and Drama Studies from De Montfort University, Leicester, and has been performing stand-up across the UK since 2011. One of her interests is experimenting with the Cumbrian dialect in her poetry and is currently working on a place-based collection exploring working class femininities. Celia once performed to an audience consisting of more dogs than people, her favourite comedian is Maria Bamford and her favourite poets include Kate Fox, Kate Tempest and Sarah Howe.

MICHAEL WORRELL hails from The Bahamas and is slowly turning into a happy icicle in the frozen north of Edinburgh. He writes primarily fantasy and science fiction, but will read whatever happens to be in front of him at any given time. If given the choice however, he will read something with dragons first, as it is the obviously superior option. His influences are more varied than he probably knows, but he likes to think that Neil Gaiman, Brian Jacques, and Ray Bradbury are among them, and suspects that several anime creators will soon join the list.

CONTACT: moworrell7@gmail.com

YANTING ZHANG is currently studying Creative Writing at The University of Edinburgh. She grew up in China, and had published several prose fictions in Chinese literary magazines, such as *South Wind*, *Man's World*, and *The Psychic*. Since writing in English, she had also won a few literary prizes, for example the Best Fiction Award of *Particle Magazine*, and the Special Mention Prize in 2016 *Nottingham Reading Scheme*. Her main topics are the social issues related to women's well-being: the glass ceiling, slut shaming, arranged marriage, enforced fertility, domestic violence, etc.

CONTACT: s1630300@sms.ed.ac.uk

THE UNIVERSITY
of EDINBURGH